THE 21ST PENNSYLVANIA CAVALRY

THE 21ST PENNSYLVANIA CAVALRY

From Gettysburg to Appomattox

BRITT CHARLES ISENBERG

THE
History
PRESS

Published by The History Press
Charleston, SC
www.historypress.com

First published 2022

Manufactured in the United States

ISBN 9781467147095

Library of Congress Control Number: 2021952406

This book is dedicated to the men of the 21st Pennsylvania Cavalry.

May their patriotism and humanity continue to inspire future generations as it has me.

…

And to my parents, Scott and Elke Isenberg:

You encouraged my interest in Civil War history from childhood and kindly continue to support it.

"Nobody said it was easy," but "lights will guide you home."

Contents

PREFACE

The American Civil War seems to be one of those enduring subjects in which many Americans can perpetually find some sort of personal inspiration or connection of interest. Remarkably, even with the consistent parade of books released every year that touch on the subject in one way or another, there are still many topics that await their "day in the sun." The story of the 21st Pennsylvania Cavalry certainly fits this category.

My personal interest in the regiment stems from growing up and living in the same geographic home as so many men who served in the ranks of the regiment. Being a "cemetery stomper," it is almost impossible for me to visit a historic cemetery in south-central Pennsylvania and not find some veterans of the 21st Pennsylvania buried there. Much to my surprise, when I first began deeply researching the unit, there was little published information available.

This particularly distressed me with regards to the regiment's first commander, Colonel William H. Boyd. The colonel achieved significant notoriety during the war from both friend and foe alike. His service spanned from near the war's opening salvo until his incapacitation by a wound that nearly killed him at Cold Harbor. Even then, he offered what little he could to the cause. His recovery was a slow and painful process. This may partially explain why a man with so many high-profile encounters has somehow escaped the history books. Boyd was also not a man to boast, and although most contemporaries held him in high esteem, reflections on his service mostly faded away with his death in 1887. That is, except for the men who served under him. However, they too were little remembered.

The 21st Pennsylvania Cavalry entered the war later than many other units. Its origin is tightly intertwined with the story of Gettysburg and its aftermath. Although it took some time until major combat finally reached the ranks, when it did, it was swift and severe. Transformed from cavalry to infantry and back to cavalry again by the end of the war, the 21st Pennsylvania Cavalry was one of the few regiments used in such a manner.

The story of these sons of Pennsylvania is a dynamic one. They served under Meade and Grant at Cold Harbor as infantry and made the last charge at Appomattox Court House on April 9, 1865, as cavalry. Comparatively, in such a short time, the losses in the ranks are astounding but not surprising. Surrounded by that loss, the men bore the trials and tribulations of combat the only way they could: fighting to the bitter end.

After the war, the veterans did their best to honor their comrades, and eventually two monuments were erected at Gettysburg to commemorate the story of the regiment. Members of the regimental association repeatedly called, and at times pleaded, for someone to compile a regimental history for posterity's sake. Unfortunately, that never happened.

My simple objective with this publication is to correct that oversight in some way. I believe that the following pages are far from the concluding remarks on the incredible odyssey of the 21st Pennsylvania Cavalry. To the contrary, hopefully new interest may spark in an old story that needed some dusting.

Acknowledgements

This publication was only made possible with the help of so many generous individuals. Sources from images to data were kindly provided by Gene Barr, Dave Eisenhart, Paul Russinoff, Sue Boardman, Debra Sandoe McCauslin, Patrick A. Schroeder, Becky Garretson Perigo, Mike Shirk, Chuck T. Joyce, Doug Sagrillo, Michael Jones and Ken Lawrence. Thank you to Andrew Dalton and Timothy Smith of the Adams County Historical Society. Thank you also to John Heiser, now retired, of Gettysburg National Military Park.

Support from several colleagues whom I also consider dear friends was also vital. Their depth of knowledge on the American Civil War is endless. Thank you to Ronn Palm of the Ronn Palm Museum of Civil War Images in Gettysburg, John A. Miller, Michael Passero and Licensed Battlefield Guides Tim Pierce, Chris Army, Bob Gale, John Vilgos and Dean Shultz.

With any project of such magnitude, certain people always rise to the occasion to offer that moment of inspiration or motivation necessary to complete the project. In the words of some great historical figure, thank you Tyler Loveless for encouraging me to finish this book. Also, to a fellow Licensed Battlefield Guide and extraordinary Gettysburg author/historian who I am lucky enough to call a friend, thank you Jim Hessler for helping me to stay focused on what's important.

To my acquisitions editor at The History Press, J. Banks Smither, thank you sincerely for believing in this project and supporting it through a challenging time. Also, to Senior Editor Ryan Finn for diligently combing through the manuscript to enhance the presentation and more eloquently craft this story, my sincere appreciation. And, to the entire History Press team, thank you for your professionalism, creativity and expertise.

Finally, to my amazing wife and daughter, who have endured literally thousands of hours of research and reading, road trips and cemetery walks. Snezana and Una, from the bottom of my heart, thank you for giving so much of your time to this endeavor with patience, grace and always more love.

Chapter 1

THE POHICK YELL

William H. Boyd

Forty-seven blue-clad horsemen plodded steadily along toward Pohick Church, Virginia, in column of fours. The road to the church was narrow and, by a gentle but constant curve to the right, seemed to melt away into the dense woods enshrouding the thoroughfare on both sides. Their uniforms were just over one month old, and it was the first time these men had ventured so deeply into the enemy's country. The ire of their homes brought them to this place, but recent events like the Federal rout on the plains of Manassas just three weeks earlier changed everything. Prior to that bloodiest battle in American history (to that time), most of these men probably thought they would never have an opportunity to see their proclaimed adversary on a battlefield. That was in the past though. All they knew was that the enemy was out there somewhere—and close, too. What that enemy looked like or how they would know what to do when they saw them were questions for their officers to grapple with.[1]

The objective was clear, to the commander at least. "Proceed on a scout down the Mount Vernon road and vicinity of Accotink, to capture, if possible, 27 cavalry of the enemy." Entrusted by division commander Brigadier General William B. Franklin of the newly minted Army of the Potomac with this assignment on August 18, 1861, was Captain William H. Boyd. He was the commander of Company C, 1st New York Cavalry—better known as the Lincoln Cavalry.[2]

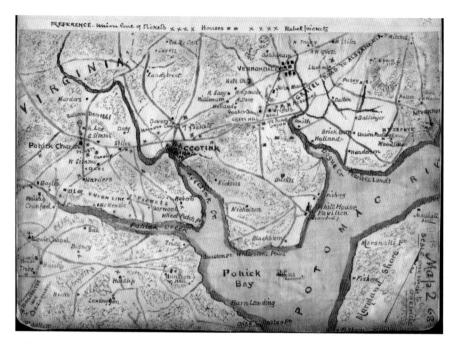

1862 map of the lower Potomac showing Pohick Church by Robert Knox Sneden. *Library of Congress.*

Upon reaching Accotink just after noon, Captain Boyd learned that the enemy was at Pohick Church, another two and a half miles farther west. Diligently, he sent three men ahead of the column to reconnoiter in that direction. As they neared the historic church, which dated to 1774, one of the scouts "came galloping back, and, in an excited manner and tone of voice loud enough to be heard by all," told Captain Boyd that an entire regiment of Rebel cavalry was waiting in the woods to ambush the party. Without any orders, some of the men who overheard the conversation "wheeled about in the road and faced towards camp," bent on removing themselves from the impending danger. At that very moment, another one of the scouts "was seen approaching at speed, waving his hat as a signal to the troop to be off," only exacerbating the panic among these greenhorn cavalrymen.[3]

Regimental historian William H. Beach correctly observed that "a little trepidation was natural," but that did not satisfy Captain Boyd, who now found himself at the rear of his column. The captain even admitted in his official report that the actions of his scouts, who "thought they discovered a whole army," caused a stampede. Luckily, the last of the three scouts and Boyd's orderly, Oliver B. Knowles, returned during those chaotic moments and completely changed the tide of the day's events. It was the first of many close consultations between the two over the coming years. Knowles informed the captain that he rode close enough to the enemy's line to count them, and he estimated that there was only a squadron opposing their approach to the church.[4]

Captain Boyd put spur to horse and, thanks to his equestrian skill, reached the head of his retreating column. He halted them with apparently little trouble and in "his manner imparted courage" with the knowledge provided by Private Knowles. Then Captain Boyd turned his men around and called up Knowles and his nephew, Sergeant William H. Boyd Jr., to his flanks. Boyd at the helm, the trio led the now steadied command back up the roadway in the direction of the church. All the while, Private Knowles kept his commander apprised of his earlier observations. The men were ordered to draw their pistols in preparation for the coming collision.[5]

Approaching the intersection at Pohick Church, a Confederate soldier issued a challenge to the head of the column. With that, Captain Boyd ordered his men to charge, and "our men shouted, cheered, and charged." Lieutenant James H. Stevenson remembered that "away they went, like a whirlwind, yelling and firing as they advanced." Stevenson also claimed that the Confederates were so surprised that they got off only one volley at

Pohick Church today. *Photo by author.*

their assailants. That volley killed Private Jacob G. Erwen of Montgomery County, Pennsylvania, the first man under Captain Boyd's command to die in combat. He was also the first Union cavalry volunteer to be killed in action during the Civil War.[6]

The Confederates quickly mounted up, but not before two of their own men were wounded by Yankee revolvers in the close-quarters fight. The Southern riders attempted their escape by using three diverging roads just beyond the churchyard. They were all successful, but not for lack of trying by Boyd's men to stop them. Small parties of Yankees pursued, "shooting as they rode," some within a short distance of Occoquan nearly five miles beyond the church, but they could not "outfoot" their well-mounted opponents, who had "very superior horses." Along with the death of Private Erwen, two other Yankees disappeared during the encounter. One eventually returned, but the other was never heard from again.[7]

The day's events were all conducted under the watchful eye of Lieutenant Charles Henry Gibson of General Franklin's staff, who accompanied Boyd's column. Lieutenant Gibson's presence and his opinions of the affair seemingly only helped in the aftermath. Although Franklin never said as much in official correspondence, based on subsequent events, he fostered admiration for Boyd's willingness to go at the enemy. Northern newspapers heralded Captain Boyd's men for their bravery in the days that followed.

During a review of General Franklin's command on August 22, Captain Boyd's company was even personally complimented by General George B. McClellan, who promised to procure them better horses, which he later did. Regardless of the commendations, Boyd's first mission was only a partial success. He effectively scouted the Mount Vernon Road as ordered but failed to bring in enemy prisoners. Maybe more importantly, a valuable lesson was learned that day, as well stated by the regimental historian: "In a fight of cavalry against cavalry the advantage is with the party that moves first. It is difficult to withstand the impetus and momentum of a well-directed cavalry charge." Because of the courage inspired by Captain Boyd that day, men who served under him would forever offer the name of their cheer during a charge as the "Pohick Yell." Indeed, with hindsight, the encounter at Pohick Church became celebrated as the first successful Union cavalry charge of the Civil War. However insignificant in the grand story of the war, the day's events were a credit to the leadership of Captain William H. Boyd and a promising sign of things to come.[8]

William H. Boyd was in many ways the prototypical American of the mid-nineteenth century. His father was a soldier in the British army, which led to his parents' emigration from Ireland to the British garrison at Quebec, Canada. William Henry was born on July 14, 1825, the first of five children. As a young man, Boyd apprenticed in printing and then published a city directory in Canada. He married Elizabeth Scott Watson in 1845. The couple then moved before 1852 from Chambly County, Canada, to the United States so that William could pursue opportunities in cultivating his directory business, which he did in New York and Philadelphia. His brothers and a nephew also joined in the enterprise, expanding directories across eastern Pennsylvania. While his career flourished, so too did the Boyd family. William and Elizabeth had six children between 1849 and 1859.[9]

William H. Boyd later in the war as a colonel. *Author's collection.*

The secession crisis of 1861 provided William with an opportunity to follow in his father's footsteps. Colonel Carl Schurz made a stop in Philadelphia in May 1861 after receiving permission from President Lincoln to raise a volunteer cavalry regiment. Learning that some locals were themselves already engaged in raising a cavalry regiment from the city, Schurz arranged a meeting. "To these he made known his appointment, and invited them to join him; assuring them that no more volunteer cavalry would be called for or accepted by the Government."

The gentlemen in attendance respectfully listened to Schurz's explanation on the current state of affairs, although all declined his invitation except for one man: William H. Boyd. After more conversation, Schurz expressed his desire that Pennsylvania should raise a battalion, "which would give her the right to a major, and also a voice in the appointment of the other field and staff officers of the regiment." Boyd pitched in with vigor to recruit a battalion, needing at least seventy-nine men for each of the four companies. It was a tall task, and in the end he did not succeed.[10]

Upon arriving back in New York, however, Carl Schurz was successful in recruiting a large contingent of German immigrants, many with prior military experience, to join his volunteer cavalry regiment. On June 5, much to the dismay of recruiting efforts, Schurz was ordered by President Lincoln to Madrid, Spain, to serve as the U.S. minister to Spain. Boyd traveled with other members of the recruiting team assembled by Schurz to Washington, D.C., and after some contentious meetings with Secretary of War Simon Cameron, they received permission from President Lincoln to finish the job started by Schurz. Colonel Andrew T. McReynolds of New York was placed in charge of presenting the unit. He is also the man who proposed naming the regiment the Lincoln Cavalry, evoking a humorous inquiry from President Lincoln: "Who christened the baby?" After being told that he called the troops out, to which the committee proudly responded, Lincoln supposedly remarked that "he was accused of being its father, and might as well own up." The name stuck.[11]

Boyd returned to Philadelphia on July 1. He immediately took possession of the cavalry barracks at Chestnut Hill with a squad of men to continue recruitment and begin drill. Together with his previous efforts, from May through July 1861, Boyd recruited more than three hundred men and defrayed their expenses out of his own pocket. Keeping these men in camp without actual marching orders proved to be a difficult task though. As other units were being raised locally, many of his recruits who were getting offers elsewhere disappeared. In fact, he lost so many that by the time orders came, he had only enough men for one company still in camp.[12]

There was more bad news. The change in leadership from Schurz to McReynolds had consequences. Although the Lincoln Cavalry was invented by Carl Schurz as a Federal regiment, his removal and the recruiting quotas that developed during that same period demanded that the unit adopt a state affiliation. Because the majority of the regiment's muster rolls comprised men from New York, they were redesignated the 1st New York Cavalry, much to the chagrin of Boyd.

There were several inquiries for the transfer of Boyd and his men to any number of Pennsylvania units, but it was too late to redistribute the Pennsylvanians. Ironically, the Keystone State ever after claimed Boyd's company as its own, naming Company C of the 1st New York Cavalry the 10th Pennsylvania Cavalry. It seems that Boyd never entirely overcame this dispute either. Other New Yorkers in the regiment later did this as well, but the captain would always sign official correspondence with his name atop the words Lincoln Cavalry instead of 1st New York Cavalry. It seemed that if the opportunity presented itself under honorable circumstances, Boyd would much rather serve his adopted home state of Pennsylvania. In the meantime, he would continue to discharge his duties honorably.[13]

Not a moment too soon, for on July 10 an order from the War Department directed the furnishing of horses and equipage to Boyd's remaining recruits upon their arrival in Washington. The time to join the fight finally arrived. Boyd was officially mustered into Federal service as a captain of Company C in the Lincoln Cavalry on July 17. His company was mustered in just two days later. Captain Boyd assembled his men on July 22 at the railroad depot off Broad Street in Philadelphia, and they departed for the capital.

Arriving at 5:30 p.m., the company went into camp on East Capitol Hill. Boyd with his two commissioned lieutenants made their way to the Willard Hotel, where they were greeted by fantastical tales of the previous day's battle along the banks of Bull Run. Despite previous illusions by so many politicians of a short war, events promised that Captain Boyd would get a chance to test the company he worked so hard to raise. The company received horses, arms and accoutrements on July 24. After three weeks of incessant drilling, Captain Boyd was granted the opportunity to take his men to the field, culminating in the action at Pohick Church on August 18. It was only the first of many brushes with the enemy to come, and Captain Boyd's reputation was already rising in the eyes of his superior officers.[14]

Besides Captain Boyd, two other men who would later have a significant impact on the history of the 21st Pennsylvania Cavalry displayed much promise in the brief skirmish at Pohick Church. Orderly Oliver B. Knowles served faithfully as a scout and provided Captain Boyd with the reliable information necessary to successfully rein in his command. He also was at the head of that first charge right next to his superior. His performance on August 18 was a foreshadow of everything that successful cavalry operations would require by the middle of the war.

Oliver Knowles was born in Philadelphia on January 3, 1842, to Levi and Elizabeth Adeline Croskey Knowles. Oliver was the second oldest of four children, and his father, a native of New Jersey, ran a respected mercantile business in Philadelphia. At a young age, Knowles was recognized for his skills as a rider. His intellectual abilities raced him through high school, and by age fifteen, he was working for his father's business.

Within a month of the opening of hostilities, Knowles enlisted under Captain Boyd, and his skills were recognized almost immediately. As an example, during the

Oliver B. Knowles later in the war as a colonel. *MOLLUS Collection.*

early weeks of the company's recruitment, Oliver accompanied Captain Boyd to the post office when the captain was summoned to another errand. Boyd asked young Oliver to remain until he could return. Unfortunately, the captain forgot about this request and went back to company headquarters via an alternative route, while Knowles remained sitting at the post office. Remembering later that day what he had forgotten earlier, Captain Boyd hurried back to the post office to find Knowles faithfully awaiting his return. Boyd was so impressed with Knowles that he asked him to serve as his orderly, to which the young man quickly assented.

Knowles was not imposing in his quiet manner, but physically he stood over six feet tall; according to a comrade, he had a "wiry, muscular frame." It was also noted that "his goodness in heart was only equaled by his courage and patriotism." Although he was not yet known to those above his captain, time would provide opportunities for that to change. Lieutenant James Stevenson later claimed to Knowles's father that he "mentioned him to the Captain for promotion. But he needed no 'friend at court,' for he earned his own promotion in the very first engagement." By the time the company moved on its first major campaign just eight months later, Knowles would be wearing sergeant's chevrons.[15]

The other man at the head of the charge with Boyd and Knowles at Pohick Church was Captain Boyd's nephew, William H. "Harry" Boyd Jr. He was born on Christmas Day 1841 and, like his uncle, reared in Canada. As a young man, he learned the trade of baking and candy making before joining the Boyd family business of publishing directories. Harry moved to New Haven, Connecticut, and after a short stay there, he eventually settled in Pottsville, Pennsylvania, where by 1860 he was in business with his uncles publishing local directories. When his uncle of the same name began recruiting Company C of the Lincoln Cavalry, Harry enlisted at the rank of sergeant. To this point in life, his fortunes very much depended on the fortunes of his relatives, and that would continue as their lives entered a new chapter in the midst of war.[16]

The Lincoln Cavalry, and particularly Boyd's Company C from Philadelphia, continued to distinguish itself in the field over the next year and a half. In fact, Boyd became so trusted by superiors that he was tasked with more difficult assignments, like searching out Confederate partisans and guerrillas. From late 1862 through the summer of 1863, that was largely his mission. Boyd tangled with famed Southerners under John D. Imboden, Elijah V. White and even John Singleton Mosby on numerous occasions. It was Boyd's command that treed Mosby at the Hathaway

Looking west from the Loudoun Valley toward Ashby's Gap near Paris, Virginia, an area frequented by Captain Boyd trying to flush out John Mosby and his men. *Author's collection.*

house near Salem on the night of June 8, 1863, although the Gray Ghost escaped again.

During the second week of June, after another expedition into the Loudoun Valley to track down Mosby, Boyd was ordered back toward Winchester with his command to the support of General Robert Milroy's beleaguered garrison. General Robert E. Lee's army of Northern Virginia was headed north to invade the bountiful Union lands beyond the Potomac River. Initially commanding the rearguard, Captain Boyd was tasked with escorting Milroy's supply train to safety. It would take him some time to catch up, since Boyd's wounded nephew Harry then had command of the train and was moving it from Winchester toward Martinsburg. The captain's wife, Elizabeth, and a daughter and son were also with the train trying to escape.

Confederates caught up with the wagons near Bunker Hill, and immediately a firefight broke out. Quickly the situation descended into chaos, and amid the gunfire, the buggy carrying Captain Boyd's family took off behind a spooked horse. The carriage was upset, although luckily none of the passengers was killed. They were taken as captives temporarily and then released. The train eventually did reach Martinsburg mostly intact.

At Martinsburg, Captain Boyd finally caught up and learned what just happened. There was no time to tarry, however. He was now in command and had to keep the wagons rolling.

There were numerous brushes with Confederate cavalry, but eventually Boyd and his men successfully got the wagons through the Cumberland Valley to the security of Harrisburg on June 16. They could not have known it, but they were only just beginning a very long month of campaigning. The cycle of war certainly had its ups and downs.[17]

Chapter 2

The Calm that Precedes the Storm

Robert Bell and the Adams County Scouts

J ust days removed from their sweeping victory at Winchester, General Robert E. Lee's Army of Northern Virginia pressed on toward Pennsylvania's fertile Cumberland Valley. This threat to the commonwealth necessitated the immediate formation of local militia to defend the southern border. In all, Governor Andrew Curtin called for sixty thousand men for the defense of the state. The turnout was generally poor because those men of military age still at home were not interested in serving the offered six-month term. Also, previously the state sent thousands of men to the war effort, and many of them were still serving in armies throughout the country. Finally, state military officials settled on semantics for the enlistment term: "the existence of the emergency," which did inspire some enlistments.

In Adams County, thirty-three-year-old farmer Robert Bell of Straban Township answered Governor Andrew Curtin's call for volunteers. Bell was born in Menallen Township, Adams County, the youngest of four children. His grandfather served as a noncommissioned officer in the Revolutionary War, and he surely heard the lore of the elder Bell's experiences. Robert's youth was fairly typical of other children of that time—working the farm and attending the district schools. He also went to Oak Ridge Academy and upon graduation continued his father's pursuits, taking over the family farm. In 1853, he married Abigail King, and by the outbreak of the Civil War, the couple had four children.

Through the first two years of the war, Bell remained in Adams County tending to his family and the farm, with one exception. During the first Confederate invasion that culminated in the Battle of Antietam, Bell enlisted as a first lieutenant with McCreary's Independent Cavalry Company, a group of local men tasked with scouting the county. His first dabble in soldiering lasted but two weeks.

The summer of 1863 brought with it an imminent threat to home and hearth that changed everything. Now the enemy was just over the mountain, and it was only a matter of time before they crossed it. Bell rode to Harrisburg, where he arrived on June 15, the day before Captain Boyd brought Milroy's wagon train into the state capital. They could not have known each other, but the two men's paths would soon converge.[18]

Robert Bell as a major in 1865. *Adams County Historical Society.*

Bell was ordered by Pennsylvania's adjutant general to return to Adams County and round up as many men and horses as possible for the purpose of scouting the southern border. This he did, expeditiously recruiting more than forty men in just a few days. Major Granville Haller of the Department of the Susquehanna was charged with the defense of York and Adams County. He arrived in Gettysburg on June 20 and held a rally at the county courthouse to drum up recruits for defending the border. On that same day, he formally commissioned Robert Bell as a captain and mustered in his Adams County Scouts for a term of six months. Thirty-three men brought their horses from home. Seven more horses were procured from their neighbors. Bell's command was attached to Major Charles Knox's department cavalry.[19]

The Adams County Scouts, or Bell's Cavalry as they became known, went into action the following day. Rampant rumors reached Major Haller and the civilians of Gettysburg that portions of Lee's army were already infiltrating South Mountain via Monterey Pass just beyond the town of Fairfield in the southwestern corner of the county. Further evidence came in the form of refugees pouring through the county toward the safety of points east. Haller took 15 of Bell's men along with a 25-man detachment

Unidentified member of the Adams County Scouts. *Author's collection.*

of the First City Troop of Philadelphia toward Fairfield. A mile east of Fairfield, they spotted approximately 160 enemy soldiers.

Interestingly, in that moment Major Haller decided to return to Gettysburg, leaving the small band of amateur soldiers under the care of Captain Bell. It was about 6:00 p.m. when Bell cautiously advanced his men within a half mile of the town and then ordered a charge. The Rebels retreated in haste through the streets, with Bell's men chasing for more than a mile back toward Monterey Pass, only slowed by the onset of darkness. The historian of the First City Troop later wrote of Bell that "he proved himself a brave, intelligent, and conscientious soldier." Bell admitted privately to his wife, "The Rebs were much frightened as we were," but the captain did not outwardly display that fear. He also accurately informed her, "I am afraid it has been the calm that precedes the storm."[20]

Bell returned with his men to Gettysburg, but they were "kept in constant motion" for the duration of the emergency. On June 23, a portion of the Adams County Scouts went out the Chambersburg Pike beyond the Cashtown Gap. Not far beyond the gap, they spotted Confederate troopers riding in their direction. It was Company D of the 14th Virginia Cavalry in the command of General Albert Jenkins. Bell's scouts quickly reined up and retraced their steps back toward Gettysburg, leaving a roadblock at the top of the pass defended by local civilians. When the Confederate cavalry encountered the barrier, shots rang out and one Southern horseman was killed. Enough blood lost for one day, Southern troops did not venture far beyond the pass.[21]

For upward of three days, Bell and his men were preoccupied with "cautiously advancing and observing" the enemy along several different thoroughfares. The commander of the department's cavalry, Major Charles Knox, thought it odd that the infantry moved alone with no cavalry in the advance. Because of this, he was led to believe that it was merely a "flanking" party. On June 26, observations grew ominous. Confederate major general Jubal Early's division of the Second Corps came tramping through the mountain, burning the Caledonia Iron Works as it passed, and streaming out the eastern entrance of the Cashtown Pass toward Gettysburg.[22]

Sergeant Adam Black of Company B. *Author's collection.*

On that very day, the 26th Pennsylvania Emergency Militia arrived in Gettysburg. Captain Bell guided the regiment of amateurs, ex-enlistees and convalescents out to Marsh Creek (west of town) to set up a bivouac. Before Bell had even left the newly established campsite, some of his pickets rode in, reporting the enemy advancing in force along the pike. He informed the regimental commander, Colonel William W. Jennings, that he would ride out to see for himself. After a brief reconnaissance, he returned and confirmed the report. He also wrote a dispatch to inform Major Haller of the developments. It was during these moments that Colonel Jennings expressed his lack of confidence in the men he commanded. The two decided that if a crisis befell the command, and it seemed increasingly likely, Jennings would lead his men north by northeast toward Harrisburg. The cavalry would withdraw through Gettysburg and exit town on the road to Hanover, which would lead them to York.

Captain Bell then departed, riding westward again along the Chambersburg Pike for nearly two miles. He continued to monitor the steadily advancing foe. Later, Bell returned once more to the camp of the emergency men and discovered them retreating via the route he previously discussed with Colonel Jennings. According to Major Haller, Colonel Jennings made this movement under his own responsibility. This left the road to Gettysburg completely open to the enemy. Now with no infantry, Captain Bell ordered his men to ride back to Gettysburg to report to Major Haller. While riding along the Chambersburg Pike, one of Haller's orderlies delivered a dispatch ordering all troops back to Gettysburg. It was clear that Haller could not hold Gettysburg with the force at his disposal, especially now that the 26th Pennsylvania Emergency Militia was retreating north of town toward Harrisburg. The major ordered his remaining men of the First City Troop to Hanover, and they quickly departed.[23]

Postwar stereoview of the Lightner Farm and Power's Hill. Just down the pike (*left*) from this house is where Sandoe was met by White's Comanches. *Michael Passero Collection.*

Bell's men checked the enemy's advance as long as possible from a distance before they, too, were forced to evacuate. The local boys left an impression on their curious neighbors as they rode into Gettysburg, warning of the enemy's impending occupation to those people who did not heed previous warnings carried through the streets. It was about 3:00 p.m., and Captain Bell "was perfectly at home on his horse and was not uneasy, keeping a very tantalizing distance," according to one Gettysburg woman. The scouts were under chase by members of Colonel Elijah V. White's 35th Virginia Battalion.

Some of Bell's men were not wearing standard-issue uniforms because of enlisting so recently, adding confusion to the chaotic situation. Apparently the captain told them, "Every man take care of himself," each of them having been informed when to rendezvous and where. The Adams County Scouts rode out of Gettysburg along the Hanover Road. Just before the party crossed the bridge over Rock Creek, two of Bell's men, Private George Washington Sandoe and William Lightner, reined their horses to the right. This took them south along Rock Creek in the direction of Mount Joy Township and their homes, nearly five miles distant.[24]

After guiding their horses along Rock Creek for some distance, they came "through the woods down by the swimming hole" east of the Baltimore Pike and "saw some Rebs coming their way," according to Lightner. "They urged their horses on a run" through a barren field of James McAllister and came to a fence, which Lightner's horse took but Sandoe's did not. Lightner rode off in all haste, while Sandoe drew his revolver to defend himself. He fired a shot at the foe, possibly for the first time, but missed the mark. An enemy horseman simultaneously responded to Sandoe by leveling his own carbine. Another shot rang out, and Sandoe fell from his saddle, dead. He was the first Union soldier to be killed at Gettysburg, leaving behind a wife of but four short months and having been a soldier for just four days.[25]

A young man named David A. Conover witnessed some of the events surrounding Private Sandoe's death. He was standing in front of the McLean house in Gettysburg that afternoon when a Confederate cavalryman reined up in front of him. "Here is the horse," said the Confederate trooper. "I've shot the rider. I am sorry, but I had to do it in self-defense." The wife of the Evergreen Cemetery caretaker, Elizabeth Thorn, was scared to the point of fainting by the same group of Confederate riders who chased down Sandoe. In her corroborating account, Sandoe's killer came trotting up to the Evergreen Cemetery when several of his comrades noticed his extra horse. They inquired after him, "Oh, so you have another one." He responded, "the ---- ---- shot at me, but he did not hit me, and I shot at him and blowed him down like nothing, and here I got his horse and he lays down the pike."

Abolitionist James McAllister, who owned the ground on which Sandoe's blood was spilled, placed the young man's body in a spring wagon. Initially, McAllister misidentified the soldier as George Hartman before another identified the remains as Private Sandoe. McAllister took the body down the Baltimore Pike to the soldier's home in Mount Joy Township. Sandoe was

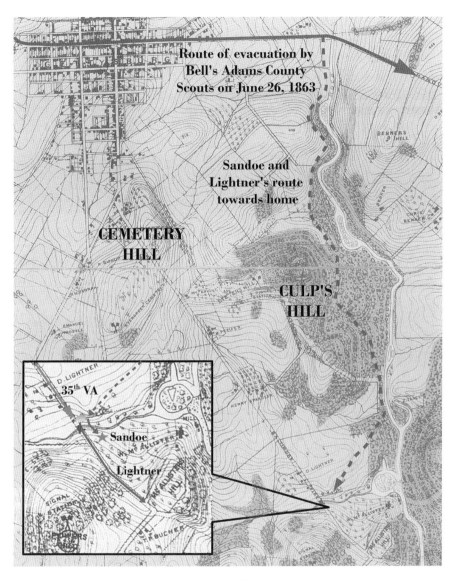

The route of Sandoe's ill-fated ride. *Map by Britt C. Isenberg.*

laid to rest at the Mount Joy Lutheran Church along the Taneytown Road, only twenty years of age.[26]

Although the greater portion of Bell's command was scattered, some men made it with Bell to Hanover and eventually York. Their efforts did not go unnoticed by locals. "The men have been performing the

Left: Jonathan H. Bosserman of the Adams County Scouts. *Author's collection.*

Right: David C. Brinkerhoff of Bell's Cavalry. *Author's collection.*

hardest kind of service," wrote one newspaper correspondent, "coming frequently in contact with the rebs, making narrow escapes and bringing in valuable information." Once in York, Major Haller continued to use the Adams County Scouts for reconnaissance until they were again driven eastward on June 27 to Wrightsville, on the very banks of the Susquehanna River. Joining them there were men from southern York County under Samuel N. Kilgore.[27]

At about 6:30 p.m. on June 28, General John Brown Gordon's brigade of Georgians attacked the defenses west of Wrightsville. Captain Bell's men, with perhaps a few hundred others, held the Confederate advance at bay for nearly forty-five minutes before retreating across the longest bridge in the world (at that time) to the safety of Columbia on the east bank of the river. As they did so, they implemented a pre-established contingency plan: they lit the bridge on fire. This was done to deny Confederates access to the eastern shore and therefore the state capital. Sixty-three years after the event, Private David E. McGuigan was remembered at his death as one of the men from Bell's command who helped set the bridge ablaze.[28]

The brief fight at Wrightsville cost Bell two more men, although both eventually returned to the ranks. Of those soldiers who dispersed at Gettysburg on June 26, some remained at home until it was safe to find their way back to the command, while others offered themselves to the Army of the Potomac just as the Battle of Gettysburg broke out in their own backyards. Captain Bell's second lieutenant, Henry G. Lott, was ordered to Virginia with a squad of men on a scouting mission by army commander General George Meade. The rest of Bell's Adams County Scouts remained at Columbia until July 11, when they were ordered to Harrisburg to join a newly authorized command.

Captain Bell wrote his wife during that time, "I had not my boots off for two weeks." It was a swift martial initiation but invaluable. Major Granville Haller later commended Bell's command, saying, "All performed their duty with commendable zeal and ability, and kept me, and therefore Maj. Gen. Couch, fully advised of the movements of the enemy. These troops were all that rendered me any assistance."[29]

Chapter 3

A LIVELY SKIRMISH

Boyd's Service in the Gettysburg Campaign

While Captain Bell's cavalry company from Adams County was scouting and skirmishing east of South Mountain, there was much occurring in the Cumberland Valley. Captain Boyd "was impatient." Now that Milroy's wagon train was safely within Union lines, the captain was ordered to take his company of the Lincoln Cavalry back into the valley to keep an eye on the inevitable approach of the enemy. His company boarded cars of the Cumberland Valley Railroad on June 19 and took the line to Shippensburg. They disembarked there and mounted up, riding about ten miles that evening to Chambersburg. On June 20, they rode to western Franklin County and arrived in Mercersburg, just ahead of a contingent of enemy cavalry. These enemy troops belonged to General Albert Jenkins's command. Lieutenant James Stevenson claimed that Boyd's men crowded into a barn and watched as the unsuspecting Southerners rode past, completely oblivious.[30]

From Mercersburg, the Yankees moved toward Greencastle, where they encamped about three miles north of the village on the evening of June 21, the same day Captain Bell and the Adams County Scouts had their first brush with the enemy on the other side of the mountain. Boyd was aware of several prowling bands of Jenkins's command, and on June 22, they found each other.

One of those bands was led by Lieutenant Joseph A. Wilson. He had two companies of the 14th Virginia Cavalry. They spotted the Yankees on a hillside. Wilson's men initially advanced with hopes of luring Boyd's men back to Jenkins's entire command, but unbeknownst to Wilson, Boyd's men already saw them coming. Captain Boyd and his men charged down the turnpike, driving Wilson's company before them—or so they thought. "The audacity with which these cavalrymen dashed towards the rebels led them [the Confederates] to suppose that they were the advance guard of a large body."

One Southern trooper with Jenkins's main body closer to Greencastle remembered hearing an "irregular, 'pop!, pop!, pop!,'" in the distance and then immediately behind their retreating comrades came the Yankees "in a whirl of dust." The race was on "through a strip of timber, down the gentle slope, over the depression, up the next rise, past a farmhouse, onto the broad level north of Greencastle," where Wilson dismounted his men now amid his own supports. From behind a fence, they turned to greet Boyd's thirty-five charging men.

Private Abner A. Arnold remembered hearing the clicking of the carbines around him as they prepared for action. He and his comrades watched three of Boyd's men ride to within twenty-five yards of the Confederate line before the Southerners unleashed a volley. A "lively skirmish ensued," and the lead Yankee was dropped from his saddle, shot in the face. At that moment, the entire 14th Virginia Cavalry went charging up the roadway, Boyd's men now in a full gallop the opposite direction.

The man killed was Corporal William H. Rihl, the first Union soldier killed in Pennsylvania during the Confederate invasion. Boyd also lost Sergeant Milton Cafferty, who was wounded and taken prisoner. One newspaper reported that five men were lost altogether. All in all, Company C was lucky to escape and fight again.[31]

Captain Boyd kept in contact with Jenkins's advance all the way through Chambersburg and back to Green Village. There was no stopping the enemy, although the Yankees did as much as they could to harass them. The Confederate pressure forced Boyd's small force back to Shippensburg by June 24. As one witness recalled, "It was warm and the dust lay ankle-deep and the painters were busy, covering with a coat of paint the words 'Union Hotel' which stood out gaunt and suggestive of the federal sympathies of mine host, upon the front wall of all the hostelry which now is called Sherman House." Apparently, the townspeople were anxiously anticipating the arrival of the enemy. "Two-thirds of the population clambered upon the roofs of houses partly because thence they could see all the fun with ease," the correspondent to the *Harrisburg Telegraph* continued.[32]

"About two o'clock Col. Boyd and his men at a full gallop sent the dust flying along Main Street, and through the town they went like the wind with

1930s view of the monument to Corporal William Rihl at the Fleming Farm. *Author's collection.*

the Confederates close behind them shouting and discharging their carbines widely [*sic*]." Ms. Eunice Stewart wrote to her parents that Jenkins's men rode into town "more like so many devils yelling like hell-hounds." Jenkins was annoyed enough that he ordered the four rifled Parrott cannons of Griffin's Baltimore Battery to unlimber on the eastern edge of town, where they proceeded to lob shells at the Yankee horsemen. "Boyd had a narrow escape on the hill east of Market Square," according to the newspaper correspondent, "for the Confederates were well within range and the carbine balls rattled around him and his little band."[33]

Boyd did not tarry long. They pressed on to Newville, thence to Mount Rock Spring, through Carlisle and New Kingston by June 27. At New Kingston, Boyd ordered Lieutenant Oliver Knowles back to Carlisle with a small party to save the military stores at the Carlisle Barracks. Unfortunately, the enemy was already swarming and kept them from achieving their objective. On June 28, Boyd was cut off by Confederates streaming toward Harrisburg, and only by riding cross-lots was he able to get the remainder of his men safely back within Federal lines. Boyd, however, was not done.

By June 29, General Robert E. Lee's Army of Northern Virginia was retracting from its advance on Harrisburg back toward Adams County. Boyd and his meager command of 120 cavalrymen were ordered out of

Charles Trump, one of Boyd's men in Company C of the Lincoln Cavalry. *Author's collection.*

the capital defenses on June 30 to probe the enemy. They moved via a circuitous route through Mechanicsburg heading west out the Trindle Springs Road. General Albert Jenkins's men had just vacated the town that morning. It is unclear whether they made contact with Jenkins's Confederates, but something caused Boyd to turn his command south onto the Boiling Springs Road and they went to Churchtown, where they encamped for the night. The following morning, July 1, they resumed their march and were "hailed to shouts of joy" upon entering Carlisle. The citizens were eager for news, but Boyd had little to report besides the fact that his command was hungry. "This announcement sent the people flying to their homes and in a few minutes the market place was filled with eatables."

Boyd remained only long enough for the men and horses to be fed. Hearing rumors that General Lee's headquarters were somewhere in the vicinity of Cashtown, the captain took his command south. They passed through South Mountain by way of Mount Holly Springs and then rode twelve miles to Bendersville, approaching Lee's sprawling army from the north. Surely the booming artillery could be heard toward Gettysburg as the troopers drew near. A major engagement was underway. This made Boyd understandably tentative, for there was no support to call on. They were alone and behind the enemy's army.

Captain Boyd temporarily split the command as they departed Bendersville to survey the road network, he leading one part and Lieutenant Oliver Knowles leading the other. Near Arendtsville, Knowles's detachment came upon Confederate forage wagons. His men quickly pounced to capture what they could. Unfortunately, the excitement of the dash dispersed the command. Within moments, Knowles suddenly found himself entirely alone—that is, until seventeen Confederate soldiers swarmed around him.

Remembering the maxim "keep the initiative," Knowles stunningly drew his revolver and ordered the would-be captors to surrender. The

Confederate soldiers likely thought him mad, but much to his surprise, they began to comply. The timing was perfect because, unknown to Knowles, the rest of his command was galloping up at his back, making for a much more menacing situation to the Southerners, who decided it best to throw down their weapons. It was a narrow escape for Knowles, but one the men were happy to write about later.[34]

The two wings reunited, and Captain Boyd led them across South Mountain again toward Shippensburg, probably bivouacking somewhere along the western base of the mountain. On July 2, eighty-eight men under Boyd made for Shippensburg and then turned south toward Chambersburg. From Chambersburg, they turned east on the road that led to the Cashtown Pass and Gettysburg. Just east of a little village called Stoufferstown, they found their old nemesis.

About seventy-five men under the command of General John Imboden were guarding wagons filled with bounty taken from the Chambersburg area. Boyd ordered his men to charge, and they captured twenty-two Southerners and thirty-three horses. On the return trip to Shippensburg, they nabbed nine more Confederate soldiers. Boyd's men then made for the mountains once again, and they encamped at Watt's Furnace, or Pine Grove Furnace, on the night of July 3. The adjutant general of the

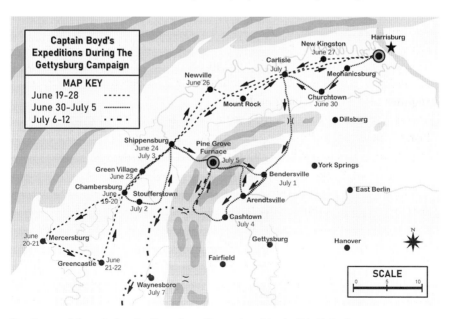

Boyd's expeditions during the Gettysburg Campaign. *Map by Britt C. Isenberg.*

department would not permit Boyd's efforts to pass unnoticed, even if he could not keep up with Boyd's whereabouts. In humble correspondence to Secretary of War Stanton, the adjutant general reported that very day, "He and his command have done good service."[35]

It was clear by Independence Day that the Southern army was moving back into the Cumberland Valley. Defeated at Gettysburg, General Lee's wounded army was making for the Potomac River. Captain Boyd gave chase. He was ordered from Shippensburg across the mountain to Bendersville and thence to Cashtown "to ascertain the movements and position of the enemy." Not far from Cashtown, his company "fell in with them" and captured eight wagons and some prisoners, pursuing the enemy through the Cashtown Gap nearly to Fayetteville. They rode into the mountains and found General William F. Smith's command of militia on July 5, which was concentrating at Pine Grove Furnace.[36]

Boyd kept in constant motion, relentlessly harassing the retreating Confederate army whenever the opportunity arose. On July 7, Boyd sent a dispatch to General Couch that read, "I was in their midst this morning, near Waynesborough." It was a short fight, but he and his men took forty-four prisoners, also reporting to Couch that the Confederate wagon train was pushing for Williamsport. Boyd then rode west toward the scene of the company's engagement two weeks before: Greencastle. After passing through the town, the column turned south and galloped through Cunningham's Crossroads. Boyd again had a sharp skirmish with about eighty Confederate foot soldiers just northwest of Hagerstown on July 9. Keeping close contact for several more days, Boyd's command was ordered to join the entire regiment at Chambersburg on July 13.

The previous two weeks were grueling to say the least for both man and horse, but Captain Boyd impressed many superiors with his tireless spirit in pursuing the enemy. He and his men rode more than four hundred miles during the monthlong campaign. Even with limited personal encounters, General Smith praised Boyd officially to General Couch, expressing that the captain "did gallant service with his small force." Boyd also impressed the local populace, who grew accustomed to his presence during the Pennsylvania Campaign. The *Carlisle Herald* described him by saying, "[T]his officer, sleepless and tireless, has merited much of this community."

Boyd's superiors eventually bestowed a just reward: his long-overdue promotion. Even that came at a price. The captain was to command a new regiment of cavalry from Pennsylvania. From Governor Andrew Curtin he requested that the officer corps comprise fellow Pennsylvanians from the

Lincoln Cavalry. With but few exceptions, his request was denied. Regardless, big changes were on the way.[37]

The captain, too, was impressed by the recent campaign with the men who served alongside him. Lieutenant Oliver B. Knowles particularly distinguished himself. Of the young subordinate's service, Boyd later glowingly stated, "It is worthy of being recorded in letters of gold. Were I to recount all that he [Knowles] did during that exciting time, I fear it would take longer to write than the campaign lasted." Knowles's star was still far from its zenith.[38]

Chapter 4

I Am Getting Fat
as You Please

Building a Regiment

While Lee's Army of Northern Virginia retreated south during the first two weeks of July, Captain Bell's company of the Adams County Scouts was encamped about one mile east of Harrisburg at Camp Couch. With them were the recruits under Samuel N. Kilgore from southern York County. Collectively, they were waiting to find out what regiment they would be assigned to. Bell's men and those serving under Captain Boyd had proven themselves efficient, resourceful and equal to the task. But for every company that amassed proficiency in the art of war through their initial exposure and thanks to solid leadership, there were three times as many that did little but congregate near the state capital in Harrisburg. To fulfill a presidential proclamation issued in mid-June, Governor Andrew Curtin called for sixty thousand men to defend the state and "to be mustered into the service of the State for the period of ninety days, unless sooner discharged." The state fell far short, raising just under thirty-seven thousand men. The new recruits were still swarming the local populace in mid-July and taxing the community's resources. Organization was sorely needed, and authorities in the Department of the Susquehanna did what they could to transfer units to other locales.[39]

Several other companies of cavalry took shape during this time. One of those was the Lancaster City Troop. Newly commissioned captain Daniel B. Vondersmith, "a most expert swordsman and horseman" from Lancaster, was given the authority by Governor Andrew Curtin to raise a company of cavalry for six months of service. With the help of his two lieutenants,

Top: Elias McMellen from Lancaster. *Matthew Fleming Collection.*

Bottom: Lieutenant William Chandler of Chestnut Level, Lancaster County. *Author's collection.*

Elias McMellen and John Killinger, the three men recruited in the city of Lancaster at the Union League Rooms, Ditlow's Hotel and Groff's Cross Keys Hotel. Word of mouth and advertisements attracted recruits rather quickly with slogans like "Young men desirous of serving their country in the cavalry, cannot do better than join this company." Recruiting progressed because of the fact that General Lee's army was, by this time, on the south side of the Potomac River and the immediate threat to Pennsylvania was quelled. By the middle of July, one hundred men were on the rolls, and the company was fully uniformed and equipped at Camp Curtin in Harrisburg.[40]

Another cavalry company from Lancaster County was formed under the efforts of twenty-two-year-old carpenter turned soldier Captain William H. Phillips of Drumore Township. Rather quickly, Phillips turned out support from the fertile planting grounds along the eastern banks of the Susquehanna River with the help of Christian Mussleman and William Chandler, who, for their efforts, were elected lieutenants of the company.

Like his commander born in Canada, Richard Ryckman of Cambria County was another young man with local ambitions who accepted a captain's commission and tallied up enlistees from his own county. In neighboring Bedford County, John Q.A. Weller marshaled men from across the county to the county seat. Weller received commendable support from Belfast-born Martin P. Doyle. The twenty-three-year-old Irishman was a cooper by trade living in Chest Springs, Cambria County, when he awoke to the new pursuit of soldiering. For reasons that are unclear, the fiery Doyle helped to round up recruits in Bedford County, but his efforts were instrumental. He was elected lieutenant for his troubles. Each of these independent commands traveled to Harrisburg.[41]

Enlistees trickled in from other locales in Dauphin, Mifflin and York Counties, but collectively they paled in comparison to the nearly 600 recruits from Franklin County. This surge of enlistees from the county most affected by the recent invasion accounted for six companies of cavalry. The benefit to these recruits was their prior military service with nine-month regiments like the 126th Pennsylvania Volunteer Infantry. That regiment "saw the elephant" at Fredericksburg and Chancellorsville. Between those two engagements, the regiment suffered more than 150 casualties. Although the 126th was an infantry unit, the combat experience and exposure to the general privations of a soldier were assets to a newly forming organization. Other experienced soldiers discharged for one reason or another came from the 77th Pennsylvania, which was serving in the western theater of the war. Officers like Josiah C. Hullinger, Arthur Bennett and George L. Miles, who had already cut their teeth on the battlefield, became invaluable. However, the future would surprise these men, who thought that they were trading their marching feet for a marching horse, making their service from late 1862 into early 1863 even more valuable.[42]

By late July, uncertainties about the reemerging potential of enemy threats from the south still distressed Governor Curtin's administration. Furthermore, riots against the national draft threatened to unhinge stability throughout the commonwealth from within. Militia units raised for aiding the emergency became problematic as well since many men were restless to go home, especially now that the crisis had passed. The administration struggled to convince these short-termers to remain in the service with Lee's army now back in Virginia.

To provide force and solution to these separate fronts, Governor Curtin decided to muster in three full regiments of cavalry to serve six-month enlistments. There were three important perks to the rollout of terms, which gained much traction for the governor. Volunteers would avoid the draft and be fully compensated, and their enlistment was only for six months instead of three years. The natural next step for state authorities was to consolidate

Top: Joshua K. Hood of Company G had previous service in the 126th Pennsylvania. *Author's collection.*

Bottom: James B. Atherton of Company D served with the 77th Pennsylvania before joining the 21st. *Author's collection.*

the independent cavalry companies ready to comply and already around the capital, thereby establishing individual regiments of twelve companies each. The result of this process was the creation of the 20th, 21st and 22nd Pennsylvania Volunteer Cavalry regiments.

Command of the 21st Pennsylvania Cavalry was given to newly commissioned Lieutenant Colonel William H. Boyd as a reward for his service through the first two years of the war. He impressed many, especially during the recent emergency. Now he finally had an opportunity to command Pennsylvanians under the Keystone State's banner. His promotion was arguably long overdue and honestly earned through much hardy service against the enemy. Upon organizing enough companies into a full regiment, Boyd was officially promoted to colonel on August 20, 1863. The establishment of the 21st Pennsylvania Cavalry could not have come at a better time for the veteran since the organizational process gave him time to recover. Boyd was temporarily out of action due to a debilitating case of the boils—no wonder after the prolonged periods of riding during the past weeks. While he could not be in the saddle, he still exercised his authority and made his first regimental command decisions.[43]

The colonel decided to take some trusted subordinates from the Lincoln Cavalry with him to the 21st Pennsylvania Cavalry. One of those men was Oliver Knowles, who became Major Knowles on August 27, another well-deserved promotion. Eventually, the major's younger brother Emerick would join the regiment as well. Boyd also invited his nephew, William Harry Boyd, to join the regiment as quartermaster with a rank of first lieutenant. Not shirking under the pressure, Harry was largely responsible for keeping Milroy's wagon train in order, which allowed safe passage from Winchester to Martinsburg before his uncle took over. Harry Boyd proved his martial capability, wounds and all.[44]

The field and staff officer positions were filled by men who collectively owned substantial experience elsewhere in the war. Welsh-born Richard F. Moson served as the adjutant of the 7th Pennsylvania Cavalry and was wounded at Lebanon, Tennessee, in 1862. He was commissioned as Boyd's second in command with the rank of lieutenant colonel. Charles F. Gillies of Philadelphia was commissioned major on account of his service in the Army of the Potomac as a captain in the 3rd Pennsylvania Cavalry, another experienced unit. The final major's commission went to John W. Jones.[45]

Of the eighteen commissioned officers from Franklin County's six companies, half of them had previous military experience, and six of them served in the 126th Pennsylvania Volunteer Infantry. Throughout the other

Martin Van Buren Coho was one of the officers with prior service experience. *Doug Sagrillo Collection.*

half of the regiment, seven officers served with other regiments prior to enlistment with the 21st Pennsylvania Cavalry and three served in militia units. There was a fair amount of military knowledge in this fresh unit, given that nineteen of the thirty-six field officers had field experience. However, the ability to meld those experiences into a flourishing regiment of cavalry would take some time.

The individual companies received their new designations and official orders informing them that they would join the 182nd Regiment of Pennsylvania Volunteers, forever known by its cavalry designation as the 21st Pennsylvania Volunteer Cavalry. The regiment was supplied with the usual array of cavalry equipage at Camp Couch. For firearms, most of the companies were issued the Whitney revolver, which had a mixed reputation. The Gallagher carbine was distributed to serve as their long arm. Two companies received Colt revolvers. After drawing weaponry, the regiment was ordered to the camp of instruction at Chambersburg.[46]

Its new camp was located a mile and a half southeast of Chambersburg on the Greencastle Road and named Camp Ferry in honor of the district commander, General Orris S. Ferry. The men quickly became accustomed to the rehearsals of drill from every page of the manual. The experienced officers continually reinforced an understanding that in all its monotony, drill was best digested as second nature for future purpose. For the recruits from Franklin County, there were plenty of temptations, especially since they were encamped amid their homes. Some of the boys did go home and were not averse to getting themselves into trouble. The proximity to home was also a blessing in disguise since family members could pay visits to the camp and alleviate some of the temptation. For the most part, discipline remained intact.[47]

The 21st Pennsylvania Cavalry was not the only regiment drilling at Chambersburg. Through early August, it was joined by four companies of the newly formed 22nd Pennsylvania Cavalry. In all there were more than one thousand horsemen with their mounts, learning the routines of mounted soldiering. In a letter to his wife, Captain Robert Bell provided the typical daily itinerary at Camp Ferry:

5:00 am—Reveille and Rollcall
5:15 am—Horses watered
6–7:00 am—Officer's mounted drill
7:00 am—Breakfast
8:00 am—Guard mounting
8–9:00 am—Officer's drill on foot with sabers
9–11:00 am—Mounted drill by companies
12:00 pm—Horses watered
11–2:00 pm—Recreation
2–4:00 pm—Non-commissioned officers drill mounted or dismounted
5:00 pm—Horses watered
Sundown—Rollcall
9:00 pm—Rollcall

Writing of the grub in camp, Bell informed his wife, "I am getting fat as you please." The transition from civilian to soldier, even for officers and men who had a taste of warfare during the emergency, was a gradual one.[48]

Lieutenant James C. Patton was one of Franklin County's own boys stationed among the familiar environs of home for training. *Author's collection.*

Like so many communities hosting thousands of soldiers for the war effort, Chambersburg and the surrounding countryside was transformed into an unpleasant environment. The only saving grace was that so many of the men residing in those newly formed martial camps were from the area and may have offered more diligence in respecting property and the citizenry. Even so, all the local sources were overburdened. Every day there were "sickening stenches in and around town, arising from imperfectly buried animals, or the filth of corrals or camps." A local newspaper correspondent pleaded that "unless some rigid sanitary regulations are speedily adopted, we may have an epidemic."[49]

The soldiers all knew that their stay was temporary and that soon enough they would be off to brave new dangers. When they eventually departed, the civilians, in many cases their family and friends, would be left to deal with the consequences of their community hosting so many soldiers. On August 20, the regiment finally received an assignment—actually, several assignments.[50]

Chapter 5

OUT OF THE FRYING PAN, INTO THE FIRE

Fall of 1863

The 21st Pennsylvania Cavalry was finally assimilated after weeks of training with the idea that they would soon get an opportunity to meet the enemy. Captain Josiah D. Hullinger's Company D was the lone exception. This company was ordered to Gettysburg on August 11 and "engaged in collecting government property" from the battlefield under the acting assistant quartermaster there. However, marching orders on August 20 took the rest of the regiment away from the enemy, but not hostilities.[51]

The regiment's marching orders were for Scranton in northeastern Pennsylvania. There they would fulfill the purpose of patrolling and restoring order to communities affected by the draft riots. In pursuance of its orders, the regiment set out from Camp Ferry via Shippensburg and Carlisle back to Camp Couch at Harrisburg. The men covered fifty-two miles in three days.[52]

On the march to Harrisburg, Captain Bell's Company B was detached and ordered back to the battle-shattered county seat in Adams County, joining Company D. Although the battle was now nearly two months' history, for district commander General Orris S. Ferry there was much disorder to contain on account of military equipment and wounded and dead soldiers. General Ferry made Captain Bell his acting provost marshal. Upon arriving in Gettysburg, Bell set up his headquarters in the office of J.C. Neely on the diamond in the center of town. Surely the boys of Company B were pleased with this assignment, as were the locals, although their proud community was a vastly different scene since the last time the Adams County Cavalry was in town.

Interestingly, although both Companies B and D were present and Captain Hullinger was the more experienced officer, Ferry confided in Bell for the job. Bell did have the senior commission of the two, but it would also stand to reason that since Company B was from Adams County and Bell was a prominent member of the community familiar with the intricacies of the local scene, Ferry believed that the captain could better press the objectives and secure the site. The *Gettysburg Compiler* reported as much, saying, "The excellent and soldierly deportment of the Company is the subject of general admiration."[53]

Captain Bell's new role was multifaceted. His men were employed in tracking down misappropriated government property for the quartermaster at Gettysburg, Captain William W. Smith. As a quasi-police force, they also had to guard all sites of military value. This included officers stationed at Gettysburg, quartermaster stores, railroad infrastructure and, maybe most importantly, Camp Letterman along the York Road. Camp Letterman was established as the first general field hospital in U.S. history. "It occupies an elevated plateau or table-land of some fifty acres, overlooking the town and the extensive battle fields for miles around." The squadron of just over one hundred men between Companies B and D commanded by Captain Bell was plenty occupied. As the captain bemoaned to his wife on August 23, "Here I am within a few miles of home and no time to get there but hope to see you all soon. I am Provost Marshall here, am always getting out of the frying pan into the fire."[54]

The other ten companies of the regiment rode on from Harrisburg. Another fifty-eight miles over three days took them to Pottsville in Schuylkill County on August 25. There they rested for three days, although their march, with the exception of one company, was far from over. At Pottsville, Captain Robert J. Boyd's Company K was detached for service quelling riotous miners. Boyd was a Franklin County merchant turned soldier with no prior military service, and his new assignment provided plenty of challenge thanks to an inhospitable local populace. The company went into camp at previously established Camp Whipple. There it remained through the winter of 1863.

Among the first lessons new troopers learned: death did not come only at the hands of the enemy, nor was it glorious. On August 26, the horse of Private "Charley" M. Ellis of Johnstown spooked, reared and fell on top of him. The young man was crushed beneath. He died shortly after the accident, the first member of the 21st Pennsylvania Cavalry to die after the regiment's formal organization. Although muster records indicate his age as eighteen years, it seems that the youngster lied about his age to enlist and was only fifteen or sixteen years old. His remains were sent home, and he was interred at Grandview Cemetery in Johnstown.[55]

The remainder of the regiment pressed on to Scranton under Colonel Boyd and settled along the banks of the Lackawanna River at Camp Cooke on August 31. The nine companies that established camp at Scranton had marched 186 miles over the previous two weeks, ten days of which were marching days. The horsemen averaged more than 18 miles per day. This was not a grueling pace by 1863 cavalry standards, but these men were not veterans. Nonetheless, still unaccustomed to their mounts and long days in the saddle, Scranton was probably a welcomed stop if not the destination they imagined when they volunteered to fight for the Union just weeks before.[56]

The horses drawn by the regiment at Harrisburg were fatigued as much as the men. The horseflesh was also detrimentally affected by a disease known as "glanders." The disease was well known long before the Civil War, but it was usually caused by the ingestion of contaminated feed or water. Symptoms in the horses could include a yellow-green nasal discharge along with ulcers on the nose. Effects on horses also included "enlarged lymph nodes and nodules on the skin" that "may look like long, hard ropes." The disease was first brought to the attention of company officers on the march to Scranton, but it affected the command through the coming fall and winter. First Lieutenant George F. Cooke of Company M noted that "glanders has raged among the horses of this troop badly. Some twenty have been killed or died from it. There were some of them affected when drawn at Harrisburg. Every effort has been made to check it but to no purpose." Similar reports survive from Companies C and E as well.[57]

The 21st was soon engaged in patrolling the mountainous environs of Scranton for draft dodgers, rioters and suspected traitors. They were an unofficial provost guard like their brothers at Gettysburg. However, unlike at Gettysburg, their show of force in such a hostile environment brimming with antiwar sentiments promised much less success. Brutal attacks by miners against their employers were common on the pages of local newspapers that September. In one case, "four Irishmen waylaid Mr. W. Peters, Mining Supt. at Stanton's Mines on the corner of Maine and Northampton street, knocking him down and literally pounding him to death with stones or slingshots." Lawlessness like this dispatched the men of the 21st to seek out the perpetrators on scouring expeditions that often concluded empty-handed.[58]

Captain Henry C. Phenicie commanded Company K, which was stationed in northeastern Pennsylvania through the fall and winter of 1863–64. *Author's collection.*

After just two weeks of this duty, Colonel Boyd received orders that would take part of the regiment back to Chambersburg. It is likely that department officials realized that Boyd was much more useful at the front, employed in his old pursuits, although it is unknown if any particular individual lobbied for his reemergence into active operations against the enemy. Regardless, Boyd led a full battalion (Companies A, F, G and I) out of Scranton on September 12 for its scheduled rendezvous with previously detached Companies B and D at Chambersburg. At Scranton, Lieutenant Colonel Richard F. Moson took command of the remaining five companies comprising the garrison to continue the often vilified work started two weeks before.[59]

Colonel Boyd's contingent arrived at Chambersburg on September 21, and the squadron from Gettysburg arrived on October 3. Upon reuniting, they were greeted with surprising news. The six companies were to be mustered out of Federal service. And so the individual companies prepared to turn over all their equipment. Several companies had completed the task of turning in their saddles and horses when they were informed that the order had been rescinded. To some of the men, this was understandably quite a disappointment. Furthermore, General Ferry could not find a suitable replacement at Gettysburg, so on October 5 Company B was ordered back to continue its work guarding the hospital. Companies A, D, F, G and I then began to move south.[60]

The men stationed in Scranton continued their monotonous duty as the days turned cooler and fall closed in on their camp along the river. The men went to work building more formidable winter quarters. They continued their scouting missions as well. Each company received independent missions from Lieutenant Colonel Moson. There were also preparations to be made in anticipation of the upcoming local elections. The Franklin County men of Company L under Captain George L. Miles arranged for an assessor to meet them at Camp Cooke. Unfortunately for the men, the assessor "miraculously disappeared" on the agreed-on date for the meeting, "he being a Copperhead and of course opposed to soldiers voting."[61]

Captain Miles and his "McClure Dragoons" persisted in the arduous mission of searching for outlaws. On September 20, tragedy struck the company. Private Nelson Lane was "for some unknown reason in the act of shooting a dog" when his older brother Henry interfered. Nelson's revolver discharged, and Henry was killed almost instantly. It is unknown where Private Henry Lane was interred after the sad event.[62]

Before the war, Captain Miles was an oyster seller, railroad fireman, baker and restaurateur living with his wife and daughter in Chambersburg, Franklin County, when the Civil War erupted. He first served for three months with the 2nd Pennsylvania Infantry. Then he enlisted for nine months as the captain of Company G, 126th Pennsylvania, and saw action at Fredericksburg and Chancellorsville. His experiences there were nothing like the events unfolding in the Scranton area that fall.[63]

On one October day, Captain Miles attempted to arrest a "disorderly civilian" when the fellow drew a revolver on him. Without a chance to inquire whether the man might reconsider, the trigger was pulled and the cap exploded. For some unknown reason, the bullet did not discharge, and Captain Miles was spared through a "narrow escape." The man was placed under guard to await trial. For the unsuccessful assassin's sake, it was well that Miles survived. The captain was deeply respected by his men. They presented him "with a handsome saddle and bridle," and Second Lieutenant John Harmony made a speech in his honor. Miles closed the ceremony by expressing his gratitude for their confidence and kindness.[64]

Fueling the fervor in tensions throughout the region was the pending gubernatorial election. Would the state continue under the leadership of Republican Andrew Curtin and support the Lincoln administration's bid for a successful prosecution of the war? Or would it vote for the Democratic nominee, "Copperhead" Judge George Washington Woodward, and give up on more than two years of sacrifice? Even though Pennsylvania was the only state in the Union that had laws that permitted soldiers to vote from outside the commonwealth in an election, this legislation was overturned, and in the fall of 1863, the men of the 21st Pennsylvania Cavalry could only send letters home to implore fellow constituents how to vote. The one company present in its voting district for election day was Company B. Ballots were cast on October 13, 1863.

With many on edge, after the final votes were tallied, Governor Curtin was declared the winner by more than fourteen thousand votes. Newspapers around the commonwealth brandished the news depending on their political affiliations. In Franklin County's *Franklin Repository*, one headline read, "All

Hail to the Old Flag! The People Vindicate Their Loyalty! Northern Sympathy Played Out! Gov. Curtin Re-elected by over 20,000 Majority!" Franklin County went for Curtin. Not surprisingly, the counties in northeastern Pennsylvania, where half the 21st Pennsylvania Cavalry was stationed, went for Woodward, as did Adams County. Regardless, President Lincoln could rest easier with victories in both Pennsylvania and Ohio. On the same page that the *Franklin Repository* issued the results of the election, it also published President Lincoln's proclamation for a national day of Thanksgiving on the last Thursday of November: "And I recommend to them that, while offering up the ascriptions and blessings, they do also, with humble penitence, for our national perverseness and disobedience, commend to his tender care all those who have become widows, orphans, mourners and sufferers in the lamentable civil strife in which we are unavoidably engaged, and fervently implore the interposition of the Almighty hand to heal the wounds of the nation and to restore it, as soon as may be consistent with the Divine purposes, to the full enjoyment of peace, harmony, tranquility and union."[65]

Meanwhile, Colonel Boyd moved with five companies (A, D, F, G and I) from Chambersburg through Greencastle to the old Antietam battlefield in Maryland, arriving there on October 18. They did not stay long, and it became evident to the men that an opportunity to see the enemy might be coming. The following day, they reached the strategic town of Harper's Ferry, gateway to the Shenandoah Valley.[66]

James Linton of Company C had this image taken while in Scranton. *Author's collection.*

Lieutenant Franklin Springer of Company A. *Author's collection.*

Shortly after entering the town, Colonel Boyd received orders to send a company of troopers into the Loudoun Valley. Boyd chose Captain Richard Ryckman's Company F for the assignment. The mission was brief, but the Cambria County boys captured three prisoners and four horses during the excursion. It was the first of many such scouting missions to come.

The regiment next moved to Charles Town, West Virginia, and the Department of West Virginia formally became its assigned area of operations. At Charles Town, Colonel Boyd was reunited with his old comrades of the 1st New York Cavalry. Surely there was much catching up, but there was little time for pleasantries. Rumors of Colonel Boyd's old adversary, General John Imboden, and his Confederates in the lower valley presented new opportunities. This also signaled that the Pennsylvanians and New Yorkers would go into action together.

The most notable of several expeditions began on October 26. Colonel Boyd, "with his usual energy," led his combined force through Berryville and White Post before turning toward Front Royal. There they engaged a brigade of Confederate cavalry believed to be under the command of Colonel Thomas Rosser. The South Fork Shenandoah River north of Front Royal was running high and unfordable with artillery, but the Federals pressed on. At Front Royal, the command diverted west toward Strasburg and arrived there on October 27. After scattering some stray Confederate soldiers and capturing a few, the colonel ordered his men to withdraw toward Winchester. They rode on to Middletown, Newtown and then Winchester before turning for home.

Boyd was clearly back in his element, and the work was fruitful. From one of the prisoners, it was ascertained that General John Imboden's camp was at Bridgewater, below Harrisonburg, on October 25. Boyd's men captured twenty-two Confederates during their foray, including one major, one captain and three lieutenants. Two of the captured officers—Captain George Washington Nelson Jr., and Second Lieutenant Thomas Hugh Burwell—were serving on the staff of General William Nelson Pendleton. Apparently, they were "rusticating among their friends in the Valley" when Boyd's men interrupted their visit. Two more lieutenants were conscription officers sent from Richmond to engage in "conscription ad libitum," according to one newspaper. They were to round up all millers, mechanics and artisans, "with the exception of one to each neighborhood." A correspondent to the *Philadelphia Inquirer* humorously concluded, "Colonel Boyd has given this well laid plan a frosty and galling nipping in the bud." Boyd's troopers also captured a "four-horse Confederate team and wagon, filled with army goods,

Samuel Mowers of Company D.
Author's collection.

valued at $10,000." The 21st Pennsylvania returned to camp at Charles Town on October 28, having "behaved gallantly" and without losing a man.[67]

Brigadier General Benjamin F. Kelley was extremely pleased by the results of Colonel Boyd's raid and officially placed him in command of the department's brigade of cavalry. This gave Boyd his former regiment, the Lincoln Cavalry, now under Major Timothy Quinn, as well as a detachment of the 1st Connecticut under Major Erastus Blakeslee, Major Henry Cole's Maryland Battalion, Company F of the 2nd Maryland under Captain Norval McKinley, Company M of the 6th Michigan commanded by Captain Harvey H. Vinton and the 1st Battalion of the 22nd Pennsylvania Cavalry commanded by Major B. Mortimer Morrow. With Colonel Boyd elevated, Major Charles F. Gillies took command of the five companies of the 21st Pennsylvania Cavalry.[68]

The Unionist populace of Jefferson County, West Virginia, also seemed pleased with the occupying force of its community. "An old and excellent officer, with a fine cavalry organization," wrote a correspondent about Colonel Boyd and his men, "well mounted and completely equipped, he will give IMBODEN, WHITE, GILLMORE and their tatterdemalions very little rest." Another paper boasted of Boyd, "He is one of the officers who will never suffer a surprise, and is just the man for a border command." Indeed, a larger operation to cripple Confederate infrastructure was being planned in the department, and Colonel Boyd was guaranteed a role.[69]

Brigadier General Benjamin F. Kelley issued orders to General William Averell on October 30 to take a mixed infantry, cavalry and artillery force on a raid from Beverly, West Virginia, toward the Virginia and Tennessee Railroad at Dublin Station, Virginia. The objective was to destroy the railroad bridge over the New River, which would sever the vital supply link between east and west.

Averell's command departed on November 1 from Beverly heading south. About halfway to the objective, the column was halted by Confederate troops under Brigadier Generals John Echols and Albert G. Jenkins, culminating in the Battle of Droop Mountain, West Virginia, on November 6. By the end of the day, Averell's men had outflanked the Southerners from their formidable position. Even in victory, however, the delay and casualties were enough to stymie Averell's raid. It was discovered on November 9 by the 8th West Virginia Mounted Infantry that Imboden's Confederates were in the vicinity of Covington, Virginia, probably moving to link up with Echols or Jenkins. This prompted a response from Brigadier General Kelley, who hoped they might be able to trap him with a force from the north.[70]

Colonel Boyd was the man selected for the mission. On Friday evening, November 6, the colonel led much of the department's cavalry up the Shenandoah Valley. They rode south through Berryville, Millwood, White Post and Front Royal. At the latter place, they learned that Imboden's campfires could be seen burning near Woodstock. Boyd did not hesitate and turned the column toward Middletown and eventually Strasburg. From Strasburg, they continued along the Valley Pike and reached Woodstock at about 7:00 p.m. on Sunday night.

As they came into town, several Confederate troopers went scurrying, and the Yankees captured eleven prisoners. Imboden's main force, however, was nowhere to be found. "Sympathizing citizens gave him [Imboden] timely notice of our advance," wrote one trooper, "and he ran away." In all, Boyd's mission captured thirty prisoners and twenty horses. His command, including five companies of the 21st Pennsylvania, covered more than 130 miles in three days.[71]

On November 11, good news arrived in the form of a commissioned officer who was new to the regiment, but not to Colonel Boyd or Major Knowles. Major Knowles's younger brother, Emerick, who was up until then serving with the Lincoln Cavalry, accepted a commission as first lieutenant in Company G of the 21st Pennsylvania. Emerick was apparently concerned about the regiment's short-term enlistment and militia designation by some sources. It is unclear what assuaged his concerns,

George W.C. Myers of Company D. *Author's collection.*

but quite possibly talk of a likely long-term enlistment was already then percolating among the regimental commanders.[72]

Boyd was again ordered out in search of Imboden the following week. He departed on November 15 with approximately seven hundred cavalrymen of the 21st Pennsylvania, 22nd Pennsylvania and Cole's Maryland Battalion, along with a section of Battery A, 1st West Virginia Light Artillery. They took with them four days' worth of rations and rode up the valley to find Imboden. The command reached Strasburg after a march of forty-one miles on the first day.

Departing at daylight the following morning, they reached Woodstock at about 10:00 a.m. Commanding the advance guard was Captain James H. Stevenson, Boyd's replacement in Company C of the Lincoln Cavalry. Suddenly, shots rang out as about twenty Confederate horsemen who were concealed on either side of the road began to pepper the Federals. It was a short fight. Captain Stevenson ordered a charge and quickly dispersed them. In the chase, which must have conjured up the old "Pohick Yell," several Confederates were captured, including Lieutenant George Christopher Hamman of Company F, 10th Virginia Infantry, and a mail carrier. However, the biggest prize was a wagon loaded with four barrels of apple brandy "intended for Imboden's camp."[73]

Although Boyd wished to feed his men, the pesky Confederate skirmishers kept his advance preoccupied, so he determined to forge ahead. Reaching Edinburg, the volume of shooting again rose. Stevenson's advance guard found a company of Confederate cavalry but again drove them "like sheep." From Edinburg, Boyd and his subordinates could see smoke drifting up from the base of Edinburg Gap in the Massanutten Mountain. They believed this to be the camp of the enemy troopers they had just driven away and decided to continue down the Valley Pike toward Mount Jackson.

Riding southward, the cat-and-mouse game continued. On one occasion, they met enemy horsemen with the saber. Captain Stevenson admitted, "The boys were so elated with their success that I could not restrain them, and on they dashed" a little too far. Boyd reported with some consternation that three of his men were captured and Private Daniel Black was killed because of outdistancing the main column.[74]

The enemy's resistance stiffened as Boyd's column approached Mount Jackson. Major Robert White of the 41st Virginia Battalion commanded the Confederate force attempting to slow the Federal advance. His command included a portion of Gilmor's Battalion, a company of Marylanders and a section of Captain John H. McClanahan's Staunton Horse Artillery.

When within a quarter mile of the town, one piece of the Staunton Artillery commanded by Lieutenant Farley Carter Berkeley fired off a warning shot against the lead Federal skirmishers. It must have made quite a spectacle since the barrel of the twelve-pound Blakely gun burst, making it unfit for further service. Boyd deployed his men into line of battle on either side of the Valley Pike and called up his section of Battery A, 1st West Virginia Light Artillery. The two guns began to fire on the town, and after only a dozen shots, the enemy disappeared from their front. Colonel Boyd believed that the enemy was "very much surprised, for they supposed we had no artillery with us." The success did come at a cost. Captain Stevenson was within six feet of Corporal John H. Hoagland, who doubled as a newspaper correspondent, when "a conical shell, fired from one of the rebel guns, struck him in the face, knocking one half of his head off, covering me with his blood and brains."[75]

Moments after Hoagland's death, Lieutenant Emerick Knowles of Company G, 21st Pennsylvania Cavalry, informed Stevenson that the enemy appeared to be retreating. The news was conveyed to Colonel Boyd, who ordered his men through town. They pursued and crossed the North Fork Shenandoah River.[76]

The Southerners made their next stand atop the next eminence around the present-day Mount Jackson Cemetery. The Federals quickly drove them across the south branch of the North Fork Shenandoah River, occupying the high ground their enemy had just vacated. The Confederate horsemen dashed through a low, flat plain known as Meem's Bottom and redeployed with waiting comrades in a formidable position on Rude's Hill, which was another mile and three-quarters distant. Major White's new position offered a sweeping vantage point of the entire plain and the lone river crossing. Boyd recognized that "unfortunately the topography of the country was such that we could not reach their guns with our own artillery until they were out of range." He was forced to be content with staring across the wide-open plain between. "I deemed it prudent not to pursue them any farther, as we were within 3 miles of New Market, and my horses were very much jaded." Dejectedly, the column turned back for Edinburg.[77]

Boyd's column was not done being harassed though. When the head passed through Edinburg, they were again fired upon by about twenty enemy troopers, possibly the same group that peppered them earlier in the day. The Southerners were more distinctive this time, however, wearing blue overcoats. Thinking they might be comrades, Boyd's men held their fire until the camouflaged foe opened on them. It did not take

Union Church in Mount Jackson witnessed the engagement of November 16. *Author's collection.*

View south to Rude's Hill and Major White's position across Meem's Bottom from Colonel Boyd's vantage point on the south side of the Shenandoah River. *Author's collection.*

Jacob G. Baker of Company I and his wife, Louisa. *Author's collection.*

the Southerners long to realize that they were far outnumbered by the Federals and put spur to horse. Despite the excitement, no one was lost. The column continued down the Valley Pike, and Colonel Boyd ordered his men to halt three miles south of Woodstock in the vicinity of Willow Grove to bivouac for the night.[78]

Just before first light on November 17, bushwhackers caused quite a commotion. The unseen enemy unleashed a volley at the tied-up horses. Luckily, because of the darkness, their aim was far too high. Still, the entire bivouac suddenly came to life, even though the pot-shotters quickly escaped on foot into the mountains. One man from Major Henry Cole's Maryland Battalion was slightly wounded. Not wanting to risk any more such agitation, Colonel Boyd got his column up and moving. After a long journey without disturbance, they arrived in Winchester that night.

Early the following morning, as they were departing for their base at Charles Town, the column was again attacked by bushwhackers concealed in a house. One member of the Lincoln Cavalry was seriously wounded. Boyd's blood was up with this lawless warfare, and he ordered a search for the perpetrators. Four men were found "secreted beneath the floor. I made them walk to camp barefooted," wrote Boyd in vengeance. "They belonged to Gilmor's command."[79]

General John Imboden, who was not present for the fight at Mount Jackson, later declared in his official report of Major White's performance that his command lost only one lieutenant and eight men, while another man was wounded and two horses killed on picket duty. Imboden also claimed to have killed eight men and wounded eighteen more Yankees. Not surprisingly Colonel Boyd's report of the expedition diverged on the casualty count, stating two men killed, two wounded and five missing. Although Imboden also asserted "the enemy got no government horses, cattle, or other property in this raid," Boyd turned in "27 prisoners [including two officers] with their horses and equipments, about 90 fat cattle, 4 barrels brandy, about 50 tents, 3 four-horse teams, and a quantity of tobacco and salt."[80]

Although they had not captured Imboden's command, Colonel Boyd's Yankees proved themselves a stubborn force to reckon with on the expedition. The operation's overall failure resulted from the fact that the intended trap was never set. The expectation of coordination with Averell's force failed. The general changed plans, and Boyd had no way of knowing. In hindsight, the colonel's decision not to press the enemy at Rude's Hill was a prudent one.[81]

Chapter 6

HE SAYS HE LIKES SOLDIERING FIRST RATE

Reenlistment and Big Events

While five companies of the 21ˢᵗ Pennsylvania were off to war in Virginia and six more were patrolling the coal region of northeastern Pennsylvania, Company B under Captain Robert Bell returned to Gettysburg as the provost guard. Arriving on October 5 in familiar environs and amid their homes, the Adams County Scouts set about continuing the guard work they previously undertook.[82]

Camp Letterman general hospital on the York Road was still the scene of suffering, dying and recovering soldiers from the great battle, now three months a memory. However, the number of patients continued to dwindle through the end of the month and into November. Indeed, local attention in Gettysburg shifted from the maimed to the dead. Pennsylvania governor Andrew Curtin visited the battlefield and, like all others, was horrified at what he observed. Many corpses, or parts of corpses, scattered the landscape for miles around. Even if they had been buried, summer rains laid waste to the shallow grave sites in many places, unearthing their macabre inhabitants.

The appalling situation compelled Governor Curtin to hire a local agent, David Wills, to see that Pennsylvania's fallen received the care and dignity in final rest they so nobly deserved for their sacrifice. What began as the commonwealth's project bloomed into a national cemetery project backed by the other seventeen Union states that had soldiers who were killed in the battle.

Seventeen acres were purchased by Wills adjacent to the town cemetery and atop the battlefield's most significant piece of real estate, Cemetery Hill. Bids were also solicited for the disagreeable work of exhuming and then reinterring the Union dead from an area covering nearly thirty square miles. The winning bid was granted a contract that paid out $1.59 for each body exhumed, examined and interred on the hill.

Out of respect for the community, David Wills requested of Governor Curtin approval for commencing the work in November, so as not to disturb the remains any more than necessary while the weather was still warm. This was granted. In the meantime, landscape architect William Saunders laid out the plan for the cemetery. The graves were to be arranged by state in a semicircle around the summit of the hill.

With pledged support from the Union states, it was decided that a dedication would be held on October 23. The delegation of states chose renowned orator Edward Everett to provide the dedicatory address. Everett replied to the proposal with one alteration, the date. He recommended November 19 instead, and so the dedications would be held on November 19, 1863. Exhumations began on October 23 regardless of the ceremonies, and the work continued into November.

Three weeks before the dedication, David Wills invited President Abraham Lincoln "to set apart these grounds to their sacred use by a few appropriate remarks." Lincoln accepted the invitation along with members of his cabinet. These consequential events transpiring beyond the purview of Captain Bell and the men of Company B set the stage for a formal honor none of them ever expected, but one that they would never forget.[83]

Being the provost marshal on the scene, Captain Bell and his Adams County Scouts were chosen as the presidential guard as long as President Lincoln was in Gettysburg. Preparations were made in advance to receive the president's entourage, although well before their arrival, thousands of civilians descended on Gettysburg, as did dignitaries from across the Union. The only recently repaired Northern Central Railway into Gettysburg was overstressed, and some visitors did not arrive in time for the following day's events.

Lincoln arrived after a tiresome journey on the evening of November 18 and was met at the train station by Major General Darius N. Couch, commander of the Department of the Susquehanna. Captain Bell's troopers were also on the scene. They escorted the president and members of his cabinet uphill, just one block south to "the Diamond," where Lincoln would spend the night at the home of David Wills. The residence of the cemetery's mastermind, a large three-and-a-half-story brick home, would eventually host more than three dozen visitors that night. Lincoln was ushered up to a bedroom on the second floor overlooking the confluence of roads, the very transportation network that brought the battle to the small town in July.

Captain Bell posted First Sergeant Hugh P. Bigham outside the president's door. At the entrance to the home was Hugh's younger brother, Rush. Not long after being posted, Sergeant Bigham received a telegram to deliver to Lincoln. Bigham rapped on the door, to which Lincoln answered and received the correspondence. According to Bigham, he left the door open and momentarily took a seat at his desk before returning to address the sergeant. "Guard, this message brought me good news. I was not sure I could come to Gettysburg because my son, Tad, was seriously ill in the White House. He improved the day before I left Washington and this dispatch tells me he is very much better. Thank God for this news. I can rest better tonight." Lincoln then went back to work at his desk.

After a short time, Lincoln requested to meet with Secretary William Seward at the Harper residence next door. Bigham led the way. The conference did not last long. Lincoln reemerged, saying to Bigham, "You clear the way and I will hold onto your coat." Arriving back at the Wills house, the president retired to his room and was not disturbed again. The Adams County Scouts remained vigilant through the night.[84]

The following morning, Thursday, November 19, a procession assembled, and the guest orators were serenaded down Baltimore Street to Cemetery Hill. Company B remained on guard duty, although there was a much larger military presence by that time that included the Marine Band, Battery A of the 5th U.S.

Sergeant Hugh P. Bigham stood outside Lincoln's bedroom at the Wills house. *Paul Russinoff Collection.*

Rush Bigham stood guard at the York Street entrance to the Wills house on the night of November 18, 1863. *Paul Russinoff Collection.*

Artillery and the 5th New York Heavy Artillery. The column arrived on Cemetery Hill shortly after 11:00 a.m.[85]

An invocation and music preceded Edward Everett's speech, which lasted almost two hours. It was about 2:00 p.m. when Lincoln finally rose and delivered his "few appropriate remarks" in front of thousands, which included Company B of the 21st Pennsylvania Cavalry. At the conclusion of Lincoln's Gettysburg Address, a salute of powder charges from the artillery rent the air. The president and his entourage were then escorted back into town by military procession. In town, Lincoln was "the victim of a 'hand-shaking' that must have tested his good nature to the utmost." Later in the afternoon, another stirring incident occurred. Lincoln attended a political rally at the Presbyterian church arm in arm with the civilian hero of the Battle of Gettysburg, John Burns. The president's train departed the Carlisle Street station at 7:00 p.m. Although he would never again visit the town that hosted the war's bloodiest battle, his words never left.[86]

While the Adams County Scouts remained in range of their homes, Colonel Boyd and the five companies with him operating in the Shenandoah were back in the saddle again. Boyd's cavalry consisting of the 21st Pennsylvania, Cole's Maryland Battalion and the Lincoln Cavalry, approximately seven hundred men total, were part of a joint expedition up the Shenandoah Valley. The infantry component commanded by Colonel George D. Wells consisted of his own regiment, the 34th Massachusetts and the 12th West Virginia, approximately one thousand men. With Wells were two batteries of artillery, the 17th Indiana and 1st West Virginia. Colonel Boyd's previous expeditions had cut deeply up the Shenandoah Valley, but no Union expedition would penetrate farther than this one until the Valley was captured in its entirety by Union forces in the fall of 1864.[87]

George D. Schriver of Bell's Company B. *Author's collection.*

Boyd's cavalry brigade departed on December 9 and rode through Berryville and Winchester and then on to the familiar environs of Woodstock by December 13, well in advance of the slower-moving infantry under Colonel Wells. At Woodstock, the vanguard, Captain Josiah Hullinger's Company D of Franklin County, tumbled into a brief street fight with Confederates. Ironically, one of the enemy insurgents was a fellow Franklin Countian. Captain Hugh Logan split loyalties with his brother and moved to the Shenandoah Valley shortly before the war began. In no time at all, the Mexican-American War veteran pledged allegiance to the Confederacy. He was notorious to the men of the 21st Pennsylvania Cavalry for having turned his back on the flag. The Rebel captain served as a staff officer and scout for none other than General Jeb Stuart earlier in the war. In fact, he helped guide General Stuart through Franklin County during his first raid into Pennsylvania in October 1862 after the Battle of Antietam.

Colonel Boyd called up the Lincoln Cavalry to support Hullinger's Company D, and the added pressure quickly helped to drive the outnumbered defenders fleeing through the streets. During the firefight at Woodstock, most of the shots exchanged missed their marks, with two known exceptions. Captain Logan was shot in the right arm and thigh by Hullinger's men, who eagerly scooped him up as a prisoner of war. Nine other Confederates were captured as well. Corporal Samuel J. Banker was the only man in Company D wounded that day.[88]

While Boyd's men continued up the Valley, Colonel Wells's infantry and artillery became bogged down due to poor weather, confusion about the roads and no guides to lead them. Boyd's troopers awaited the infantry, only making small incursions while six days whittled away. Finally, on December 19, they continued. The column pushed southward to Harrisonburg, where rumors quickly caused Wells to wonder if they had gone too far. Deserters and prisoners informed him that Brigadier General Thomas Rosser's Confederate cavalry were breeching the valley via Ashby's Gap and that General Fitzhugh Lee's brigade was also approaching. Furthermore, General Jubal Early's division was supposedly camped at Mount Crawford, only nine miles distant.

Boyd and Wells consulted about the threat and decided it best to withdraw the infantry back to New Market while Boyd's cavalry screened the enemy. It proved wise, as Early's division advanced to Harrisonburg on December 21. While Wells took the infantry down the Valley, Boyd and his troopers skirmished with the Confederates all the way back to Mount Jackson. The column was by then well on its way back to Winchester, where Colonel Wells's infantry and artillery arrived on December 23. The colonel closed his commentary on the expedition saying, "The men are in excellent health and spirits, and averse to halting to-day. They want to get home. Some, however, are very foot-sore and many barefooted." The cavalry contingent reached Charles Town on Christmas Eve "to enjoy their merry Christmas," having covered nearly two hundred miles in fifteen days.[89]

Captain Robert Bell's Company B spent the remainder of November and much of December in Gettysburg. One notable effort, under the direction of Lieutenant James Mickley, was honoring their fallen brother, George Washington Sandoe. Mickley, with the help of First Sergeant Hugh P. Bigham, secured eighty dollars in donations and then appointed Second Lieutenant Henry G. Lott and Sergeant Cyrenius H. Fulweiler to procure a memorial stone to place over Sandoe's grave

Lieutenant James Mickley, Captain Bell's second in command. *Author's collection.*

at the Mount Joy Lutheran Church. In this effort they were successful, and the memorial stood over Private Sandoe's grave until just before Memorial Day 1999, when a new stone was erected in his honor.[90]

Events seemed to portend a joyous holiday at home. However, it was not to be. On Christmas Eve, the Adams County men received orders to march across South Mountain and report to Greencastle in Franklin County. That Christmas morning was a typical soldier's Friday. The men in the ranks dispensed with any thoughts of celebration and rode out of Gettysburg. They arrived in Greencastle after a nineteen-mile march. Captain Bell wrote for everyone when he said to his wife, "I suppose your Christmas was like mine not very pleasant." Fortunately, he at least was able to get up to Chambersburg for a holiday dinner, the lone joy of the day. It did little to brighten his outlook though, and the captain could think only of his family. "I think I can see you seated around the stove with Nannie and Martha playing and Willie waddling over the floor," he wrote.[91]

For all the disparate parts of the 21st Pennsylvania Cavalry, be they in Virginia, Franklin County or near Scranton, it was time to begin soul searching about their brief service with the regiment. The officers of the regiment were notified that they could begin recruitment of the regiment for three years if they wished to continue serving. As a new year dawned, the six-month enlistment was rapidly nearing the end. Some of the men in the ranks had already answered the call to serve their country twice.

Through the regiment's service thus far, there was generally more danger from disease and accident than the enemy. How long this fortune could persist remained to be seen. Private Ambrose J. Price of Captain Miles's Company L wrote to his cousin Sylvester, who was a draftee serving in the 149th Pennsylvania, that he "likes soldiering first rate." With a bit of good-natured cynicism, cousin Abraham of the infantry noted, "If he had to carry the knapsack on his back,

Philip A. Snyder of Company B. *Author's collection.*

he would not like it quite so well—especially if he had to march day and night as I have had to so." There was no denying that fact. The regiment was ordered to rendezvous at Harrisburg for the purpose of recruiting for a three-year enlistment. There was, however, still work to be done elsewhere.[92]

Colonel Boyd's detachment of the 21st Pennsylvania Cavalry stationed at Charles Town was never far from the enemy. The harsh winter weather compelled Confederate general Robert E. Lee to dispatch several brigades from General Jeb Stuart's cavalry division to the Shenandoah Valley in order to procure enough forage not only for man but for beast as well. This did not go unnoticed. One force under General Fitzhugh Lee threatened Winchester in the first week of the new year, 1864. Although the movement by Lee was truly more of a foraging expedition, it concerned Union department commander General Kelley that a more ominous enemy incursion might follow.

In response, General Kelley ordered Colonel Boyd out on January 3 to make a reconnaissance toward Winchester. Boyd had with him about three hundred men. Shortly after departing Charles Town, the command began to receive reports that a large body of the enemy was in Winchester. Boyd split the command as they approached the town. Charging in from the north, east and south, the Yankee troopers surprised a few Confederates milling about the town. "A perfect skedaddle took place," wrote Colonel Boyd. "We captured 6 and killed 1, and mortally wounded a Captain Armstrong." Boyd learned that General John Imboden's force of about eight hundred, in this instance commanded by Colonel George Imboden, was encamped on the road to Cedar Creek at Kernstown. The Yankee troopers rode on to Kernstown only to discover that they had withdrawn once again. Boyd skirmished with Imboden all the way to Newtown.[93]

At Newtown, another noteworthy event occurred. General Jubal Early's respected scout, Captain John C. Blackford, and three of his men "stopped at a public house in Newtown to warm themselves." Soon thereafter Sergeant Charles N. Warren and Private John Hogan of the Lincoln Cavalry, who were dressed in Confederate uniforms, entered that same public house, which was known as "Aunt Mary's." Discovering Blackford and his posse inside, the two disguised troopers departed and reported their findings to the vanguard of Boyd's column. Sergeant Edwin F. Savacool, commanding Company K of the Lincoln Cavalry, rode ahead with Warren, Hogan and five other men.

Blackford and his party were alerted to the approaching Federals and exited the building to take cover in the garden out back. Savacool's men showed up moments later and entered the house. They inquired where the Rebels went, but Aunt Mary "stoutly denied having seen them." Savacool stormed through the lower floor of the house and, seeing no sign of the foe, stomped into the garden out back. Fearing they were trapped, Blackford and his men made a run for their horses. The entire group mounted successfully. Savacool's men were in the saddle just as quickly, and a running fight with revolvers ensued. Only one man was hit. It was Blackford, and his wound proved to be mortal. Colonel Boyd had Blackford's body taken back to Jefferson County and was quoted in the *Richmond Dispatch* as saying, "[H]e was a brave man, and deserved an honorable interment." That was the extent of the excitement at Newtown before Colonel Boyd broke off the engagement with Imboden. It was the second time in as many months that the colonel's men extinguished the careers of infamous enemy scouts.[94]

The colonel also learned from locals and prisoners that

Lee's and Rosser's cavalry had avoided Winchester, and gone toward Moorefield, W. Va., and to Paw Paw tunnel, for the purpose of destroying it. Lee had Walker's [old Stonewall] brigade of infantry with him, in all about 3,000, two or three pieces of artillery, and some wagons. Early's division never came any lower down the valley than Middletown, and were there last night when I left Newtown. He has a large wagon train, artillery, and about 5,000 infantry. A report was prevalent and seemed to be well-founded that Fitzhugh Lee's forces were expected in Winchester at any moment, and this gained some credit with me, from the fact that numerous signals were exhibited—rockets and firing of guns (small).

David B. Timmons of Company D. *Author's collection.*

His small command far outnumbered, "I prudently retired to Charlestown, arriving in camp at 3 a.m. [January 4], having traveled over 60 miles in seventeen hours."[95]

Unbeknownst to Colonel Boyd, the same mission that found the five Charles Town–based companies of the 21st and him responding to the enemy near Winchester also initiated the deployment of a sizeable portion of Company B of the regiment from Greencastle, Pennsylvania. Second Lieutenant Henry G. Lott took twenty-three men to guard the Potomac River fords between Hancock and Clear Spring, Maryland. Nothing came of this venture, but previous enemy raids prompted a more vigilant response. Regardless, the river was too high for an enemy crossing.[96]

The Confederate cavalry force under General Fitzhugh Lee did make it to Moorefield, West Virginia, and captured a significant Union supply train with artillery ammunition and cattle at New Creek Depot. Lee also determined that there was "very little supplies to be obtained" for the army in that area. Although the expedition was a disappointment from the Confederate perspective, if Lee would have known how much alarm he caused Union forces, he surely would have been pleased.[97]

Colonel Boyd went back to Winchester with his brigade of cavalry, but on January 10, 1864, the 21st Pennsylvania Cavalry received its marching orders for Harrisburg. On that very day, one of the units that had served with the 21st Pennsylvania since its arrival at Charles Town was attacked by Mosby's partisan rangers at Loudoun Heights. Major Henry Cole's Maryland Battalion fought off the surprise attack and could claim a hard-earned victory, but it was a stark reminder of how unexpectedly the relative calm could be reversed. There were big events awaiting the Pennsylvanians at home too. The 21st Pennsylvania Cavalry was to play the role of honor guard once more.[98]

After Governor Andrew Curtin's important victory in November, his second inauguration was to be held in Harrisburg on Tuesday, January 19. His victory was an important one for the Lincoln administration and the prosecution of the war to a conclusion, whatever the result. Because the governor and the war were inextricably linked, the inauguration ceremony itself was planned with a show of force in mind. All those units that could be spared for the day were made available from the Department of the Susquehanna.

In the case of the 21st Pennsylvania Cavalry, it was convenient to order its participation since it had to return to the state for recruiting duty and the discharge of those not reenlisting. All but three companies of the regiment stationed at Scranton reached the state capital in time for the grand occasion. For Captain Bell's Company B, the boys from Adams County held quite a high bar in terms of expectations, especially after their experience in November 1863 at the Gettysburg National Cemetery dedication.[99]

The military procession gathered at eleven o'clock that morning on Market Street, and the 21st Pennsylvania Cavalry, colors flying, was sixth in line behind quite an esteemed group of individuals. The department chief, Major General Darius N. Couch and his staff, along with Brigadier General Julius Stahel and staff, led the way toward the governor's mansion. The hero of Gettysburg, Major General Winfield S. Hancock, and his staff were behind them with Battery E of the 5th U.S. Artillery and five different military bands. After picking up Curtin and his entourage at the gubernatorial residence, the impressive column marched to the state capitol, where the parade orderly fanned out around a beautifully decorated large semicircular wooden platform erected for the ceremony. The platform was decorated with regimental battle flags and, apparently, several captured flags from the enemy.[100]

Once the commotion of the crowd settled and everyone was in their place, a prayer was offered, and then Governor Curtin was sworn in for his second term. The oath of office finished, Governor Curtin stood in front of the large gathering and pledged anew his responsibilities to the state and federal constitutions. He then spoke eloquently about all that had transpired since his first inauguration:

> *Three years of bloody, wasting war, and the horrible sacrifice of a quarter million lives attest the desperation of their purpose to overthrow our liberties....Our people have been sorely tried by disaster, but in the midst of the deepest gloom they have stood with unfaltering devotion to the great cause of our common country. Relying upon the ultimate triumph of the right, they have proved themselves equal to the stern duty, and worthy of their rich inheritance of freedom....In this great struggle for our honored nationality, Pennsylvania has won immortal fame. Despite the teachings of the faithless*

and the hesitation of the timid, she has promptly and generously met every demand made upon her, whether to repel invasion or to fight the battles of the Union whenever and wherever her people were demanded. Upon every field made historic and sacred by the valor of our troops, some of the martial youth of Pennsylvania have fallen.

The governor then spoke directly to the men in uniform. "I beg return to the generous people of my native State my hearty thanks for their unfaltering support and continued confidence. They have sustained me amid many trying hours of official embarrassment. Among all these people to none am I more indebted than to the soldiers of Pennsylvania, and I here pledge to those brave men my untiring exertions in their behalf, and my most anxious efforts for their future welfare, and I commend here, as I have frequently done before, those dependant [*sic*] upon them, to the fostering care of the State."

Upon the conclusion of Curtin's inaugural speech, which was "responded to with the wildest enthusiasm," a fifteen-gun artillery salute was fired. Then a grand review was held in front of the capitol on State Street. The governor supposedly sat on a platform behind the desk on which the Declaration of Independence was signed as the 21st Pennsylvania Cavalry and several other units marched past. The festivities in Harrisburg continued long into the evening, although for its part, the 21st Pennsylvania retired to its campsite east of the city.[101]

The following morning, the men were ordered to Chambersburg. "We have consecrated a cemetery and inaugurated a Gov.," wrote Captain Bell to his wife, "and that is as much as you could expect of us....Yesterday was a big day at Harrisburg, like the 19th at Gettysburg." In a separate letter, the captain indirectly alluded to the one thing on everyone's mind: "Some of the boys say that they are going to keep us in to inaugurate Old Abe and then we will be all around the big things." Company B could lay claim as the only company of the regiment to witness both momentous events, but whether it fully appreciated it or not, the entire regiment was on the stage of history. The question that now vexed the men was: who would stay the course by reenlisting?[102]

Captain Bell himself "spent a good many sleepless hours in thinking over this thing and it never went harder with a husband to tear himself from a dear and loving wife and children." Such was the case for so many. Whether it was purely bluster to entice those on the fence to make a decision or reality, local newspapers reported, "[W]e are glad to learn

Lieutenant Howard B. Jeffries and Helen, the bride he found while stationed at Scranton. *Author's collection.*

that most of the men will re-enlist for three years." The *Franklin Repository* went further in its compliments not only of the unit in general but also of Colonel Boyd, saying, "Col. Boyd is a superior officer, and will be held in grateful remembrance by the people of the border for his services during the last six months." The one prediction all the men of the regiment could guarantee if they decided to reenlist for three years was that there was no avoiding the elephant any longer. The chances of their participation at the seat of war, especially after Colonel Boyd's performance in the Shenandoah Valley, were quite high.[103]

Chapter 7

VERY MUCH DISCOURAGED

Spring of 1864

B y mid-February, the regiment was encamped four miles west of Chambersburg, where the Loudoun Turnpike (modern Route 30) crosses Back Creek. Three cavalry regiments under Brigadier General Julius Stahel were stationed in and around Chambersburg. Recruiting was conducted vigorously to fill the ranks for three-year terms in all three regiments. Although the invasion was six months in the past, the memory of the enemy bringing the war to Pennsylvania motivated men along the border with Maryland to enlist. However, many of them had already done so during or shortly after the emergency concluded.[104]

Still, in the 21st Pennsylvania Cavalry, the companies were filled nearly to capacity. Less than half of the company officers decided not to reenlist. They included Captains John Q.A. Weller, Samuel Walker, Arthur Bennett, Robert J. Boyd, George L. Miles and Lieutenants Samuel N. Kilgore, John Killinger, Isaac Cramer, Christian Musselman, William P. Skinner, Robert G. Ferguson, William F. Peiffer and Warren M. Foster. The reasons for heading home varied from age and health to personal business that demanded their attention. Several other officers transferred to different units or reenlisted again later with ambitions for promotion.[105]

Recruiting was carried out as far away as Philadelphia. The lone known Jewish officer of the 21st Pennsylvania Cavalry, First Lieutenant Benjamin J. Levy, had a station set up in the city on Chestnut Street. Levy served with the regiment as commissary officer from its inception until being transferred to the U.S. Commissary Department only days from the war's end. Levy's

Conrad K. Stumbaugh of Company D chose not to reenlist but still ended up serving again with the 207th Pennsylvania. *Shippensburg Historical Society.*

recruitment endeavors in Philadelphia were almost certainly fueled by the city's connection to Colonel Boyd and its association with the now well-known Company C of the Lincoln Cavalry.[106]

February 20 was a busy day in Chambersburg. The six-month men who chose not to reenlist from all three regiments stationed there were formally mustered out of Federal service. All companies in the 21st Pennsylvania Cavalry were successfully recruited to their allotment, and the new three-year regiment was officially mustered into Federal service the same day. The complement of officers included many six-month veterans, but the transition to new officers was still significant. It should be noted that even though some men were serving as lieutenants, captains and majors at reenlistment, in some cases they did not receive their commissions until April or even July. The regimental line officers as of that day are as follows:

Field and Staff:
Colonel William H. Boyd
Lieutenant Colonel Richard F. Moson
Major Charles F. Gillies
Major Oliver B. Knowles
Major Robert Bell
Adjutant Henry C. Pearson
Quartermaster George Fleming
Commissary of Subsistence Benjamin J. Levy
Sergeant Major Henry B. Kendig
Surgeon William H. King
Chaplain Isaiah L. Kephart
Chief Bugler John Kadel
Regimental Saddler Theodore F. Colby
Veterinary Surgeon Peter Gockley

Company A:
Captain Hugh W. McCall
First Lieutenant Daniel V. Pruner
Second Lieutenant Franklin Springer

Company B:
Captain James Mickley
First Lieutenant Henry G. Lott
Second Lieutenant Isaac W. Bucher

Company C:
Captain Daniel B. Vondersmith
First Lieutenant Samuel T. Kleckner
Second Lieutenant Benjamin H. Ober

Company D:
Captain Josiah C. Hullinger
First Lieutenant James C. Patton
Second Lieutenant David L. Pislee

Company E:
Captain William H. Boyd Jr.
First Lieutenant Martin V.B. Coho
Second Lieutenant Richard Waters

Company F:
Captain Richard Ryckman
First Lieutenant J. Speer Orr
Second Lieutenant Thomas D. Black

Company G:
Captain William H. Phillips
First Lieutenant Emerick Knowles
Second Lieutenant William Chandler

Company H:
Captain Charles W. Palmer
First Lieutenant George F. Cooke
Second Lieutenant Samuel Henry

Company I:
Captain Elias McMellen
First Lieutenant Martin P. Doyle
Second Lieutenant Thomas H. Wellstead

Company K:
Captain Henry C. Phenicie
First Lieutenant Lewis H. Henkell
Second Lieutenant George W. Kennedy

Company L:
Captain John H. Harmony
First Lieutenant Wilson H. Reilly
Second Lieutenant John T. Pfoutz

Company M:
Captain Richard W. Hammell
First Lieutenant Albert T. Clark
Second Lieutenant John A. Devers

Although there were some new faces wearing shoulder straps throughout the regiment, Colonel Boyd and his subordinates used their time in Chambersburg wisely, constantly drilling so that everyone could become accustomed to their new roles. Also, with proper permissions, the line officers did what they could to allow the men who discharged their duties appropriately the opportunity to visit home. It was common just as well for wives and family members to be visiting the camp. "The camp of the 21st is one of the best I have ever seen," claimed a newspaper correspondent from Lancaster. He continued: "The company streets and parade grounds are cleanly swept every morning and the tents properly aired. Of course under such regulations the 'sick list'—perhaps to the chagrin of the excellent Surgeons—is a very small one." Clean or not, men continued to wilt under the strains of outdoor camp life being exposed to the elements both good and bad. One of those was twenty-eight-year-old Private John F. Romsey of Company I. He died on March 23 before ever witnessing the "glories" of a battlefield.[107]

March and April 1864 were busy with training for what was surely to come. As winter melted into spring, everyone was certain of one thing: the fighting would continue. The questions that remained unanswered were what part the regiment would play and exactly where it would be sent. Those answers would arrive soon enough.

On the last day of March, the regiment attended a formal flag presentation to accept its regimental colors. The presentation speech was made by a correspondent of the *Repository*. After the ceremony, the regimental officers hosted a ball at Franklin Hall, "which was beautifully decorated with evergreens and national flags, for the occasion." The Carlisle Barracks Band serenaded the attendees, and everyone "separated satisfied with the pleasures of the evening."[108]

Chaplain Isaiah L. Kephart. *Author's collection.*

At the front, big changes were being made in terms of leadership and strategy. Recently promoted Lieutenant General Ulysses S. Grant, the victor from the west, had just arrived at the Army of the Potomac's winter encampment in Culpeper County, Virginia. In his charge now were all Union forces in the field, and he went to work developing a strategy for victory over both General Robert E. Lee and the Confederacy.

The plan undertaken would stretch across four fronts, with the main thrust against Lee's army, hopefully turning him out of his defenses along the Rapidan River and interposing between his Army of Northern Virginia and the Confederate capital at Richmond. However, Grant mixed no bones about Meade's true objective: "Major-General Meade was instructed that Lee's army would be his objective point; that wherever Lee went he would go also."

Simultaneously, the Army of the James under General Benjamin Butler was to advance up the James River and threaten the enemy capital from that corridor. Major General Franz Sigel's Federal forces were to advance up the Shenandoah Valley, once and for all eviscerating that breadbasket of the Confederacy and threatening Lee's left flank from that direction. Finally, Major General William T. Sherman was to advance through northwestern Georgia and capture Atlanta in the enemy's heartland. If success could be achieved on several or all of these fronts, the Confederacy would surely be brought to its knees. At the end of March, General Grant requested all the troops that could be furnished to the armies for the impending campaign. On April 16, Grant reiterated orders to his commanders.[109]

To many officers in the 21st Pennsylvania Cavalry, it could hardly have seemed likely that the regiment would end up in any theater but the Shenandoah Valley. There were several reasons for this, not the least of which was the well-known exploits of its colonel in the vicinity through the first three years of the war. Furthermore, it was the closest theater of operations and imperative to the Confederate war effort. Still, time whiled away. "When I look at them drawn up in line it makes me feel sorry," wrote Major Bell to his wife, "that in a short time from now so many brave fellows from disease and hardships and battle will never return to their homes, but such will be the case owing to this horrid rebellion and the contest for the sustaining of Freedom and Justice."[110]

One of the men who reenlisted for three years, Adam Kadle of Company L. *Author's collection.*

Now and again there was excitement in camp. Private Samuel P. Glass wrote to his wife on April 29 that part of Company B was sent to Greencastle to chase down a horse thief. He related that Corporal Washington Spertzel and Private James D. Ross continued the pursuit for a mile and a half toward the Mason-Dixon line, discharging their weapons five times, although they missed their target. The thief made it to Maryland with government property in tow, and he surely was not the only one.[111]

The Army of the Potomac moved to action against Lee's army on May 4, and the spring campaign was underway. The 21st Pennsylvania still had no ideas officially where it was going, but it was just as well. The regiment was not fully equipped with arms and horses. A newspaper correspondent divulged to readers that some companies were deficient by thirty to fifty horses. Then news arrived that Colonel Boyd was leaving the regiment under special orders from the War Department to report to General Sigel in the Shenandoah Valley. It seems that Brigadier General Jeremiah C. Sullivan "formed a very high opinion of Boyd, during the fall of 1863," and recommended him to General Sigel for the coming campaign. Trusting Sullivan and his own knowledge of the colonel's previous record,

Sigel specifically requested Boyd to command part of his cavalry force for the operation.[112]

The plan was for Sigel to move with his force of infantry up the valley proper behind one detachment of cavalry while Colonel Boyd led a force of about three hundred men up the Page (or Luray) Valley to screen the infantry's left. The forces were to rendezvous at New Market. Boyd's command comprised men from several familiar regiments, which included Cole's Maryland Battalion and his old comrades of the Lincoln Cavalry. New to him were men from the 1st New York Veteran Cavalry and the 21st New York Cavalry.

The command left Winchester escorting a wagon train to the rear late on May 8 as far as Bunker Hill. The following morning, the train continued toward Martinsburg to procure supplies, while Boyd's horsemen departed for their mission to screen Sigel's left. When they arrived at Berryville, they learned that a squad was captured by some of Mosby's men, and Boyd dispatched some men to find the partisans. They came up empty-handed but remained in the environs that night. On May 10, the command crossed the Shenandoah River and rode over Ashby's Gap, where they encountered some of Mosby's men. Again the vanguard chased them on through Paris, Upperville and Rector's Crossroads. They killed one man and captured about a dozen, according to Captain James H. Stevenson.

Boyd determined to push on to Salem Depot, where the command spent the night. They rode through Manassas Gap to Front Royal the next morning, at which point Boyd forwarded their captives to Winchester. On Friday, May 13, they finally entered the Luray Valley and rode on to the valley's namesake. When they arrived at Luray, they found "a large quantity of Confederate quartermaster's and commissary's stores, which we destroyed," although many of the men made a point of nabbing a bite to eat for themselves. Boyd stayed only long enough to destroy the stores, and then the command rode up the eastern flank of the Massanutten Mountain into New Market Gap, where they found wagons laden with goods destined for enemy camps, which they promptly confiscated.[113]

Upon reaching the gap, Boyd and his subordinates had a good look into the valley proper beyond. Captain James H. Stevenson reported to Boyd the movement of what he believed were enemy troops marching from Mount Jackson toward New Market (north to south). Expecting the arrival of Sigel's force, Colonel Boyd disagreed with the assessment and thought that surely the captain was mistaken. Boyd ordered an advance down the mountain. His vanguard noticed artillery and cavalry moving toward the base of the mountain in the vicinity of the area they had to traverse and again reported the movements to the colonel. According to Stevenson, Boyd seemed "little staggered, but concluded to proceed."

The column reached the base of the mountain and arrived at a bridge across Smith's Creek, where it noticed some pickets who appeared to be wearing Federal uniforms. The pickets quickly disappeared to the opposite side of the bridge without firing, and Boyd persisted in believing they must be Sigel's men "who had not been informed of our approach." However, the colonel's senses were setting off alarms. He held another brief consultation with his subordinates, and they determined to cross the bridge and then move north by west to gain the Valley Pike as it runs into New Market. "Then, if they were the enemy, we could show them our heels and bid them defiance." Unbeknownst to the Yankees, they were stepping into a well-laid trap by the enemy. "On the Federal regiment came," wrote Lieutenant Colonel Charles T. O'Ferrall of the 23rd Virginia Cavalry, "in utter ignorance of the mistake they were making."

They no sooner got across the bridge when they heard the "well-known 'rebel yell,' accompanied with a shower of bullets." It was the 23rd Virginia Cavalry of General John Imboden's command that rose to surprise them.

Smith's Creek battlefield from Yellow Cliffs on Massanutten Mountain. The scene of the disaster is at the bottom of the photo, where the modern bridges cross Smith's Creek. The town of New Market is on the high ground in the background. *Author's collection.*

Soon thereafter, two guns of Captain John McClanahan's Staunton Horse Artillery opened on the Yankees, and although they initially returned fire, they were heavily overmatched. It was these Confederate artillerymen and cavalrymen the Yankees had spied moving toward the base of the mountain only a short time before.

"Two pieces of artillery began to send grape and canister at short range through our ranks," wrote Corporal Charles R. Peterson. "Our three hundred men stood firm, awaiting their attack until they were close upon us." The 18th Virginia Cavalry then moved to outflank them, sealing Confederate success. Boyd "behaved splendidly in the fight," trying to rally his men, but many ran for the creek and made for the western contours of Massanutten Mountain. Others charged into the face of the enemy and were quickly swallowed up. Although Boyd ordered his officers to rally those fleeing, it was a futile effort. Making matters worse, in the confusion it began to pour down rain. In moments, Boyd and his men still on the scene were doing everything they could to avoid capture. It was every man for himself.[114]

The Yankees first had to get back across the creek. The Confederates continued to fire away from the far bluff and pursued, but onward the desperate Yankees rode. Once across Smith's Creek, the survivors turned northward along the lower slopes of the mountain, forced to ride a gauntlet until they reached the relative safety of the mountain timber farther up the now drenched and slippery slope. Finally, mercifully, it appeared as though the Confederates had called off their pursuit, but Boyd and his men continued riding. By this time, much of the command was scattered to the wind.

It was after midnight when the skies finally cleared, and for a few moments, the small gang of escapees rested along the roadway. Captain Stevenson recalled how much the calamity stung Colonel Boyd when the colonel told him "he would rather have been killed than to have had such a misfortune." It was the colonel's first undeniable defeat, and he was "very much discouraged." There was little time to sulk though. The officers had to literally kick the exhausted men to wake them up and get them moving. It was still unknown how many men were captured or just lost on the mountain while trying to evade capture.

Eventually, Boyd's small posse entered the Fort Valley, likely by way of Mooreland Gap. They continued north and entered the Edinburg Gap shortly before sunrise. Not knowing what might await them on the west side of the gap, especially after the previous evening's hard lesson, Boyd decided to go up to the top of the mountain ridge and await the first rays of light so they could get a look at the valley below. As the first light illuminated the valley floor below them, a collective gasp of relief rose from the group. Sigel's entire infantry force carpeted the landscape around Woodstock just to the north. Quickly they made their way down the mountain.

The Shenandoah River was swollen from the previous evening's deluge, and Boyd and some others perilously tried to swim their horses across. Others constructed makeshift rafts. Of the 300 men who started on the expedition with Colonel Boyd, at least 125 were lost, and it probably seemed like more since individuals and small scattered groups did not return until days later.[115]

Boyd learned what caused so much confusion and surprise when he finally met with General Sigel. They may have spotted Union soldiers from New Market Gap the night before, but most of the troops they saw were probably Imboden's Confederates. Sigel discovered that General John Imboden's Confederates were blocking the path of the army south of Mount Jackson and realized the trouble it would make for Boyd attempting to come into the valley behind enemy lines. In turn, Sigel ordered his cavalry commander, General Stahel, to send relief. A detachment of 250 men from the Lincoln Cavalry was ordered to Mount Jackson, where they would rendezvous with Major Timothy Quinn's 50 men and proceed from there.

While awaiting the arrival of the 250 men sent him, Major Quinn reported he could hear the sound of gunfire in the distance, but Imboden had established his defensive position on the often used and formidable Rude's Hill between Mount Jackson and New Market, which barred Quinn's path. Unfortunately, in the rain and with light fading, the two commands never united. Quinn withdrew to Edinburg, adhering to his orders from General Julius Stahel.

Furthermore, General Sigel dispatched a fifty-man contingent of the 20th Pennsylvania Cavalry under First Lieutenant Norman H. Meldrum of the 21st New York Cavalry to find Boyd's command and order the men back to Woodstock with the rest of the army. This command was gobbled up by a small force under Major Harry Gilmor in the Fort Valley. Boyd was flying blind, his own interpretations of the situation when he departed long outdated.

It is clear in hindsight that there was also no comprehension of just how many men Imboden had at his disposal, although estimates range up to two thousand. Even if Quinn and Boyd could have reached each other, a combined force of six hundred made the situation no less perilous. General Imboden summed up the fight pretty well in his message to Major General

John C. Breckenridge at Harrisonburg: "We pitched into him [Boyd], cut him off from the roads, and drove him into the Massanutten Mountain.... They are wandering in the mountain to-night cut off." On May 15, Sigel's army was soundly defeated by that of General Breckenridge at the Battle of New Market. There was plenty of blame to share among Federal commanders from top to bottom, and it was only the start to a bleak period in the Shenandoah Valley for Federal hopes of success there.[116]

A dejected Colonel Boyd was ordered back to his regiment at Chambersburg. Captain Stevenson closed his passage on this episode with a fair analysis: "Boyd has been censured for this affair, but it is not easy to see how he could have acted otherwise than he did. A more timid man would have turned back, probably, and after all would have fared no better. If Boyd made a mistake, it was one that only a bold brave man was likely to make; and it is better to meet with disaster while boldly advancing, than while beating a retreat at the bare sight of the enemy." Still, the lonely trip back toward the Potomac River must have done little to ease the bite of that Friday the thirteenth past. Despite the disappointment, Boyd's new regiment finally received marching orders for the front.[117]

Chapter 8

SOLDIERING WITH A VENGEANCE

Cold Harbor

T he stakes could not have been higher in May 1864, but one thing
was certain, if only to the Lincoln administration. In General
Ulysses S. Grant, they finally had a commander who was going to
charge ahead to the bitter end and do everything in his power to achieve
ultimate victory. In this context, then, maybe it is no surprise that the 21st
Pennsylvania Cavalry was ordered to Washington, D.C., to eventually join
the Army of the Potomac at the front instead of points elsewhere. The only
exception was Company D, which was ordered to Pottsville to continue the
work of quelling draft opposition.[118]

The regiment left Chambersburg with about 1,100 men at 6:00 a.m.
on May 16 and after almost four days on the march arrived at Camp
Stoneman near Washington on May 19. Anticipation of what was to come
lifted the spirits among the rank-and-file, and despite some rainy weather,
the regiment was excited to be in the nation's capital. That evening, they
marched through the city "with our Band playing and Colors Flying right
past the White House and up Pennsylvania Avenue past the Capitol." After
passing the next two nights at Camp Stoneman, the troopers were ordered
to Camp Casey, and the news they received there was deflating.[119]

"An order has been received requiring the regiment to turn over all the
horses, and cavalry arms and equipments, and report to Gen. Casey. The
object of this order is to convert the 21st into infantry, and has caused much
dissatisfaction among the officers and men, who protest earnestly against it."
Major Bell was so sickened that he told his wife, "I have not had the heart to

First Sergeant Frederick W.
Shinafield of Company L.
Author's collection.

write to you." The idea to dismount the 21st was broached directly from the army chief of staff, Major General Henry W. Halleck, in correspondence to General Grant. Halleck curtly emphasized in his query that the regiment was composed of "raw recruits and of little use as cavalry."[120]

In response, Colonel Boyd attempted to pull any strings he could with hopes of a recension of the order. One of the men he reached out to was Major General William F. "Baldy" Smith, with whom he had served during the Pennsylvania Campaign. "To-day we were ordered to turn in our horses and arms and to-morrow to draw muskets and act as infantry," wrote Boyd. "I have been in the cavalry service now nearly three years, and have done as much as many other officers more favored. I feel the humiliation very sorely. Can you do anything for me? Can you have my regiment ordered under you, or even have myself with you? I am anxious to be doing something....If you can do anything for me with General Grant I will ever feel grateful."[121]

The general feeling among the regimental officers was that they were being punished for something. Even the regimental surgeon, W. Howard King, got into the mix. "For God's sake get my regiment mounted," he wrote to Colonel H. Biggs in Washington. "It is dismounted for no offense." He then sent another missive and offered Major General Smith as a character witness for Colonel Boyd. Although no known correspondence exists, surely Colonel Boyd must have wondered if the order resulted from his failure in the Shenandoah Valley just more than a week before.[122]

"No one can judge the dissatisfaction this worked in the hearts and feeling of every member of the regiment," wrote Benjamin Franklin Starner of Company B. "All discipline was lost. The men broke ranks, invaded the sidewalks, whooped and yelled like Indians....There was not an officer of the regiment who felt like attempting to command." Colonel Boyd, who journeyed to the capitol separate from the regiment, met his men in camp. "When he appeared the men rushed toward him yelling like savages, without reason or respect. The field and line officers gathered around him in silent salute. The colonel spoke not a word, but wept like a child." Among the few words remembered from the colonel during his incident, to Chaplain Isaiah L. Kephart, Boyd spoke apologetically, saying, "I did not think when I invited you to the brilliant dash on the enemy's lines that we should be treated in this manner."[123]

Despite the discontent this episode created, it is doubtful that the order was issued as a rebuke leveled at Boyd's performance. Indeed, no evidence has been found to suggest that. Besides, the failure at New Market was not Boyd's alone, and he had a long list of successes before that, which even at worst could balance the events of May 13, 1864. Boyd's superiors still held the colonel in high esteem, as evidenced by later events. It seems more likely that the army simply needed more infantry, disappointing as it was. Also, horseflesh was becoming ever more difficult to procure, and there is no doubt that the cavalry corps was in dire need of good horses for its veteran troopers. Still, this was no consolation to the men of the 21st Pennsylvania Cavalry, now dismounted. It was especially distressing to those men who were mounted on horses from home. Not only had they offered their services to the country, but now they lost an important family asset. Only some men would recoup the financial loss.

On May 23, the regiment marched to Camp Albany on foot without horses or cavalry accoutrements. There the men began drilling as infantry. The only silver lining was that several of the line officers and numerous members of the rank-and-file had previous experience serving in the infantry, which made the transition a bit smoother if not less disgruntled. Two days later, they were issued Springfield rifles, new cartridge and cap boxes, bayonets and all the other accoutrements of a foot soldier. But there was little time to practice with them. The following day, the 1,038 men of the 21st Pennsylvania Cavalry marched to Alexandria, Virginia, to embark on river transports that would take them down the Potomac River and eventually to the Army of the Potomac.[124]

From the steamer *Emily* on May 27, Major Bell wrote to his wife of the journey out onto the Chesapeake Bay: "On one side as I write you cannot discern any land and on the other side you can just discern land, everything is interesting to us that never were on the big water before." He also mentioned that a man from Company H fell overboard the night before and "boats were lowered and they could not find him although he was heard to call for help several times." The man was twenty-seven-year-old Private Samuel Fix, and the incident occurred within view of Mount Vernon. The flotilla took the regiment to Port Royal, about a dozen miles below Fredericksburg on the Rappahannock River.[125]

The regiment remained at Port Royal until May 31, when it began marching south as the guard for four hundred wagons. The men reached the Pamunkey River that night. It must have been a trying experience for men so used to riding just a week before. Special Orders Number 148 issued from the Headquarters of the Army of the Potomac reached them in bivouac, which assigned the regiment to the Fifth Corps. The regiment broke camp on the morning of June 1 and pressed ahead to join the Fifth Corps at the front near Cold Harbor. It arrived early in the afternoon.

While the 21st Pennsylvania was making its way to the field of operations, the Army of the Potomac was attempting to sidestep General Robert E. Lee's Army of Northern Virginia after several severe engagements. Much had happened over the course of the previous three weeks. From the outset, the army's command structure was tenuous at best. General Grant decided to make his headquarters with the Army of the Potomac instead of in Washington as most people expected. Meade awkwardly retained command of the army in Grant's omnipresence.

Although Grant was complimentary of Meade in correspondence with Washington, especially in the campaign's early days, the chain of command functioned under much duress, and some believed injuriously to Meade's reputation. "I see one of the newspaper men is puzzled to know what share we each have in the work, and settles it by saying Grant does the grand strategy, and I the grand tactics," wrote General Meade to his wife. With chagrin he continued, "Coppee in his Army Magazine says, 'the Army of the Potomac, directed by Grant, commanded by Meade, and led by Hancock, Sedgwick and Warren' which is a quite good distinction, and about hits the nail on the head."[126]

Adding to the relational strains were the unforeseen and often unexpected twists of a campaign. When General Grant ordered General Meade to make his initial move out of Culpeper County on May 4, the army got caught by the adversary in the dense thickets around the Wilderness Tavern, resulting in a bloody two-day struggle that was inconclusive. Grant ordered Meade to disengage and tried to move east by south to get around Lee's right flank, but the Confederates won the race. Around the tiny hamlet of Spotsylvania Court House, Grant tried to penetrate Lee's lines for nearly two weeks. Outcomes varied from utter failure to partial success, but Lee's veteran soldiers were able to recover at every turn despite an immense toll in casualties.

Amid the ongoing combat, both armies were already suffering from staggering rates of attrition. Before the campaign began, General Grant requested any garrison troops who could be spared from across the north to join the army. Although some supplemental units arrived in the form of heavy artillery regiments, these additions barely made a dent in the gaping hole.

Also, attrition did not just result from battle casualties. Looming only months away, the manpower crisis was exacerbated by the fact that thousands of Union veterans were due to muster out of Federal service at the expiration of their three-year term, having chosen not to reenlist. The Union war effort was sliding precariously toward a crossroads that directly affected the country's ability to wage war. The only silver lining was that the Confederacy shared the same struggle to an even greater extent. Furthermore, there was also a presidential election in six months that could destroy the hopes of a Republican administration's successful prosecution of the war.

As Meade put it, "We shall now try to manoeuvre again, so as to draw the enemy out of his stronghold, and hope to have a fight with him before he can dig himself into an impregnable position." On May 21, Grant ordered Meade to follow through and attempt to get around Lee's right. Despite the attrition and repeated unsuccessful attempts to break Lee's lines, the Federal army was getting closer to Richmond.

The army's next move to the North Anna River resulted in an awkward tactical disposition for both armies at times. After two days of prodding and more casualties, Grant ordered Meade to sidestep the enemy to the south side of the Pamunkey River. This move necessitated a change of base from Port

Regimental Commissary Sergeant William H. Pfoutz. *Author's collection.*

Royal on the Rappahannock River to White House Landing on the Pamunkey. Although the men of the 21st Pennsylvania could not have known it when they started tramping south from Port Royal, their marching orders were dictated by this very change of base. As the two armies jostled for positions, a major cavalry clash broke out at Haw's Shop, which led to an infantry standoff along the banks of Totopotomoy Creek the following day. The first day of June 1864 found both armies concentrating around Bethesda Church and, eventually, Old Cold Harbor. It was into this complex situation that the 21st Pennsylvania Cavalry arrived.[127]

Colonel Boyd's first mission upon arrival was to ride over to army headquarters. After a short interview with General George Meade, Boyd learned that the regiment would fight with Colonel Jacob Sweitzer's Second Brigade under Brigadier General Charles Griffin's First Division, Major General Gouverneur K. Warren's Fifth Corps. Sweitzer's brigade was composed almost entirely of veterans. Quite a number served in almost every major battle with the Army of the Potomac at places like Fredericksburg and Gettysburg. In fact, some of these men fought across this very same ground in the summer of 1862. The new brother-regiments for the 21st Pennsylvania Cavalry included the 62nd Pennsylvania, which hailed from the western part of the commonwealth; the 9th Massachusetts; the 22nd Massachusetts; the 32nd Massachusetts; and the 4th Michigan. Surely the veterans looked at the dismounted newcomers with skepticism, and who could blame them? Like every set of newcomers, they would have to prove themselves.

The change in scenery was striking to the men of the 21st. No longer were there any cultivated fields or unmolested woodlots. The landscape was a tortured mishmash of dusty open fields crisscrossed by heavily timbered woodlots, all interlaced with trenches and every kind of earthwork imaginable. Major Bell recognized, "A little rain would be a blessing to this country just now as the woods are all on fire and the whole country is one of dust, you cannot see 50 yards in any direction for dust. You can imagine how uncomfortable it is." Not to mention the season, their new brigade mates knew all too well of the miasmic airs of the Virginia Peninsula. They also knew that many of their new comrades would succumb to swamp fever before the bullet.

By the evening, the regiment was exposed to its first rain of iron. Confederate shells dropped around them sporadically, doing little damage but impressing on them the importance of having cover. "A party of us had walked about 200 yards from our camp down the road and there were two shells lit within fifty yards of us," wrote Major Bell. "We concluded as we were not wanted there we might as well leave."[128]

The regiment, with the entire division, became part of the army's right flank near Bethesda Church on the morning of June 2 when General Winfield S. Hancock's Second Corps was shifted behind the army's line southward to become the left beyond Cold Harbor. Initially, the Federal troops around Cold Harbor under Generals Hancock, Wright and Smith were going to attack that same day. However, because of the long march and the condition of the troops, Grant ordered Meade to postpone the attacks until the following morning, a costly delay.[129]

Severely weathered gravestone of Lieutenant Richard Waters at Covenanter Cemetery, Scotland, Franklin County, Pennsylvania. *Author's collection.*

Within minutes of arriving at their newly assigned position as Griffin's reserve brigade, the 21st Pennsylvania went to work digging near a copse of woods. "In a short time we had a pretty good line of works," wrote one man, "although the Rebs tried to stop our work by shelling us." Most of the shells exploded harmlessly away from the men, except for one.[130]

Near the boys of Company E, an exploding shell sent a fragment tearing through the neck of Second Lieutenant Richard H. Waters. He was dead almost instantly, the first commissioned officer of the 21st Pennsylvania Cavalry to be killed in action on the second day at the front. Waters, only twenty-five years old, was married since February. His remains were returned to his young bride in Scotland, Pennsylvania. Another young man, eighteen-year-old De Forest Pratt of the same company, was also wounded in the blast and died two and a half weeks later. This was but a preview of the days ahead.[131]

The regiment was shifted around several times throughout the night. Several Confederate attacks struck the lines, and since Sweitzer's brigade was the reserve, it was moved to threatened points though not engaged. Also, General Warren was trying to stretch his Fifth Corps line southward to bridge the gap between Bethesda Church and the Cold Harbor sector, which thinned the whole battle front. "Our brigade was moved at a double quick to all unprotected parts of the lines, and kept busy," wrote the regimental historian of the 22nd Massachusetts. At one time, Sweitzer's brigade was the very right end of the Union army's line, before moving back toward its original position along Old Church Road near Bethesda Church and attempting to get some rest.

Sleep must have been hard to come by since it rained much of the night, and only several hundred yards distant, the smattering of rifle fire continued well after sundown. General Robert E. Lee's veterans were on the move and trying to outflank Grant's positions at Bethesda Church. The veteran division of General Robert Rodes was the cause of the ruckus that night, sparring with elements of Ambrose Burnside's Ninth Corps and General Warren's Fifth Corps until finally ceding further combat to the darkness.[132]

Unbeknownst to the Union men around Bethesda Church, the Army of the Potomac's Second, Sixth and elements of the Eighteenth Corps repulsed several attacks around Cold Harbor throughout the day, and brief success on June 1 proved the weakness in the tenuous Confederate line. Although Grant delayed attacks on June 2 in order to ensure the availability of enough firepower, the situation galvanized Grant's resolve to apply the pressure on the morning of June 3 with attacks across the entire line. The main assault was to be spearheaded by the Second Corps from Cold Harbor, with support from both the Sixth and Eighteenth Corps. Burnside's and Warren's men around Bethesda Church were to threaten Lee's left flank with the hope that Lee might pull troops from there to stop any Federal breakthroughs west of Cold Harbor. The Confederate line was nearly seven miles long and, as Grant believed, must be brittle. He believed this was his opportunity to once and for all rip into Lee's veterans and deal a decisive blow.

The fight began in earnest early the next morning "with an awful roar of artillery and musketry" from the Federal left around Cold Harbor. The Second, Sixth and Eighteenth Corps attacks were underway. That was also the signal for the Ninth and Fifth Corps to attack, but it was not until almost two hours later, after 6:00 a.m., that attacks from the Bethesda Church sector finally moved forward. General Ambrose Burnside's Ninth Corps lashed toward the Confederate divisions under Robert Rodes and Henry Heth. Colonel Sweitzer was ordered to move forward and establish a connection between Burnside's left and the rest of Griffin's division. As one member of the regiment offered, "[N]ow came some hard work for the 21st."[133]

Sweitzer's brigade started its crawl out of the earthworks and into the open space beyond which was an old "orchard at the farther end of which the enemy had established his line, which was in the edge of a wood." The Confederate trenches were only a quarter mile distant. The 22nd Massachusetts and 4th Michigan led the way as brigade skirmishers. Colonel William Tilton of the 22nd Massachusetts, who was commanding the skirmish line, declared the enemy fire "as galling a musketry fire as I ever experienced on a skirmish. The men availed themselves of fences, trees, and old outhouses in the clearing for protection." The remaining regiments formed into line of battle closely behind. The exact regimental alignment is unknown, but it seems likely that the 9th and 32nd Massachusetts initially occupied the flanks with the 21st Pennsylvania Cavalry in the center.

The brigade initially marched forth "under cover of the timber on the right and somewhat lapped upon Willcox's division." However, the farther into the opening the men went, the more exposed they became, and soon enough "a perfect storm of shell, grape, canister and musket balls" greeted them. One member of the 21st remembered the dread of that moment, saying, "The screaming of our own shells combined with the thunder of the Rebel batteries and musketry, was enough to make the stoutest heart tremble." The brigade line soon jumped forward on the run, driving Confederate skirmishers of Rodes's Division before them and back toward their own earthworks.[134]

Just as quickly men began to fall out of the ranks. Blacksmith Jacob Lear of Company M was hit in the left leg, the bullet shattering the bone. He did survive to return home to Shady Grove in Franklin County, Pennsylvania, but the wound he received charging the enemy entrenchments near the Shady Grove (or Shady Grove Church) Road troubled him for the rest of his life. Sergeant Darling J. Vincent of Company C was hit in the hand and later died from complications involving his wound. Also of Company C, Corporal William H. Sutton was shot in the thigh. Daniel H. Ney of Company I was severely wounded in the right arm, which he would lose later to amputation. Austin C. Eckley of the same company was shot in the face, although he would survive his painful wound for fifty-eight years.[135]

Urging his men across the open space, Captain William H. Phillips commanding Company G was wounded by a shell fragment that ripped a hole in his side. He was removed from the field and made the long, painful journey home. The captain seemed to be recovering at times and lingered for more than a year and a half before eventually dying from his wounds on January 4, 1866, only twenty-five years old. First Sergeant Emmett D.

Captain William H. Phillips of Company G. *Michael Jones Collection.*

Reynolds of Strasburg, Lancaster County, was shot in the right side of his mouth, knocking out all the teeth in his upper-right side along with some on the bottom. Lieutenant Colonel Moson made a narrow escape as the bullet meant for him killed his mount. "In the charge they poured grape and cannister into us awful," wrote Major Bell to his wife. "I can scarcely see how I escaped.…This is soldiering with a vengeance. There were several shells struck within a few feet of me and one exploded right over my head, wounding two men right beside me."[136]

Casualties were heavy in the other regiments of the brigade as well. The regimental historian of the 22nd Massachusetts claimed a loss of one-fourth of its men in the attack. "But not a man stopped," wrote Lieutenant Wilson H. Reilly of Company L, "not one quailed, but onward we pressed and gained all that was required of us." After advancing about six hundred yards, the brigade line reached a series of enemy earthworks just vacated. They quickly discovered, however, that this was an outer line of works. Fleeing Southerners jumped behind the shelter of another line of earthworks closer to the Shady Grove Road.[137]

Now afforded some protection by the reverse slope of the enemy's outer works, the entire brigade halted to reorganize. Colonel Boyd continued to encourage the men. "Such coolness and bravery as was shown by him that day has seldom been witnessed," wrote Lieutenant Reilly. Just a few moments later, he was "sitting down cheering his men and smoking his pipe," though still in an exposed position. The bullets "flew around and about him like pelting hail." Suddenly, with a *thwack*, he was hit in the right side of the neck. The bullet just missed his carotid artery. It then ranged downward and lodged in a vertebra. The colonel immediately lost the use of his right arm. Boyd continued to give orders but had to be removed from the field "almost completely exhausted from loss of blood." The now twice dismounted Lieutenant Colonel Richard F. Moson took command.[138]

To the left of the brigade, much of Brigadier General Samuel W. Crawford's division melted away under fire, exposing the left flank of

Sweitzer's brigade to a crossfire. Luckily, several heavy artillery regiments held firm, and support from General Lysander Cutler's division drove the threat back. While the brigade was pinned down, several men noticed fire coming from the upper story of a barn close to the enemy's line. Colonel Sweitzer called forward the 5th Massachusetts Battery, commanded by Captain Charles Phillips, to extinguish the threat. Firing over the heads of their comrades, one gun turned the barn to splinters on the third shot.[139]

The brigade could go no farther, and the 21st Pennsylvania Cavalry with its brother regiments held on to their gains through the middle part of the day, when General Grant called off any further attacks. The company commanders took roll of those still with the regiment and began to tabulate their losses. Company I sustained some of the greatest losses in the regiment. Captain Elias McMellen recorded that 2 men were killed and 9 were wounded, including Lieutenant Martin P. Doyle. The entire regiment lost 8 men killed and 47 wounded. The entire brigade lost 216 men. Lieutenant Reilly wrote to the folks back in Franklin County that "[o]ur Regiment has been complimented by all the general officers in the Corps, and well may they do so, for to send a body of men in such a place when they have never been drilled one hour in infantry movements was a cruel test."[140]

On the army's left, Federal attacks were mostly stunted with ease by Lee's veterans. Yankee dead and agonizing wounded in heaps scattered the open no man's land between the lines. More than six thousand Federal soldiers were killed, wounded or missing after the morning's work. Private Henry F. Charles of Company C wrote of the scene, "Some of the dead were bloated so bad that the buttons tore off their coats. All of us that had blankets took them to cover the dead next day and shoveled a little dirt over them and that is all the burial they got. It was too horrible for a human to behold and what we tell human ears cannot understand." No easier tactical victory was had by the Army of Northern Virginia during the war.[141]

The following morning, the 21st Pennsylvania Cavalry advanced toward the Shady Grove Road to establish a picket line and discovered the Confederates were gone. Poking around the surreal scene, the men of the 21st Pennsylvania discovered what was a Confederate battery position during their charge across the field the morning before. Twenty-six artillery horses lay dead on the scene, which the regimental historian of the 22nd Massachusetts understandably claimed was testament to the abilities of their brethren from the Bay State whom Colonel Sweitzer called up to silence the

Pennsylvania Monument at Cold Harbor National Cemetery on which are etched all the units from the Keystone State that participated in the battle, including the 21st Pennsylvania. *Author's collection.*

sharpshooters in the barn. Their reconnoitering was suspended at 9:00 a.m., and they returned to their original position.[142]

The action near Cold Harbor became desultory, and the wounded lay between the lines until June 7. Meanwhile, Grant enacted his next move. The 21st Pennsylvania was part of a brigade reconnaissance out on the Shady Grove Road on June 5 and, after a brief but uneventful encounter with the enemy, marched toward Cold Harbor, where it arrived at eight o'clock the following morning. The men set up camp and lounged around through the rest of the day, enjoying the much-needed respite. Early on June 7, they marched to the Chickahominy River near "Sumner's Lower Bridge" and went to work fortifying the site. There they would remain until June 12, fronting the old Gaines's Mill battlefield of 1862.[143]

Meanwhile, the wounded were shuttled rearward for transports north if they were well enough to travel. Colonel Boyd's wound was initially reported as mortal, although he continued to cling to life through the month in immense pain. Eventually, he was transported back to his Franklin County residence just outside Chambersburg at Federal Hill. There were five months of excruciating suffering ahead. It took four separate attempts to remove the bullet from his spine—all the while, his right arm remained paralyzed. Although the brave colonel's service was not yet finished, his journey with the 21st Pennsylvania Cavalry was over after one battle.

There could be no doubt that his men greatly admired their commander, even inspiring a poem after the Battle of Cold Harbor by Lieutenant William Chandler of Company G.

> *Our chief is away from the scenes of war,*
> *From the hearts that would shield him—afar, afar,*
> *And tears in the eyes of his veterans stand*
> *As they gather together a hearty band,*
> *Our chieftain and leader in many a fray*
> *The hearts of his heroes are saddened to-day.*
>
> *His courage inspired a thousand as one,*
> *'Twas only to say, and the victory won.*
> *Hope whispers still to his sorrowing band,*
> *Once more in our ranks our leader may stand.*
> *And the foeman again to their terror shall know.*
> *The strength of his arm, as they sweep on the foe.*

God grant that from endearments of home,
Revived in his strength our leader may come,
To gladden our hearts as together we stand,
In the noblest cause for heroe's command,
To battle again our country to save
And bury rebellion 'neath liberties wave.[144]

Chapter 9

REMEMBER CHAMBERSBURG!

Petersburg

Grant once again was shifting his base and decided to move the Army of the Potomac swiftly across the James River, with his sights set on the vital logistical center of Petersburg, about twenty-five miles south of the Confederate capital. The operation was impressive to say the least, and with proper concert of movement, Grant hoped to take the city before Lee could react and support the small force left to defend Richmond under General P.G.T. Beauregard. The 21st Pennsylvania was crammed aboard transports and crossed the James River near Wilcox's Landing on June 16. From there, it marched toward Petersburg, not stopping until after midnight. "Old U.S. is after something which you will hear of pretty soon," wrote Lieutenant Wilson H. Reilly.[145]

This time, General Grant's plan was not immediately suspected by Robert E. Lee, and the "Cockade City," as Petersburg was known because of the rosettes worn by its Revolutionary-era Patriots, was ripe for the taking. Grant planned to use the Eighteenth Corps and the Army of the Potomac's Second Corps for the initial strike. There were just more than two thousand of Beauregard's men defending the city at that moment. Still more of his dispersed command was at Bermuda Hundred. The main advantage for Petersburg's overextended defenders was the imposing Dimmock Line, an extensive series of field fortifications about ten miles in length around the city.

Major General William F. "Baldy" Smith's men of the Eighteenth Corps, after hours of delay, finally engaged the scant group of Southern defenders late in the day on June 15 and captured nearly a mile of the impressive fortifications. Confederates in that sector, however, fell back to an interior line just as substantial. The vanguard of the Second Corps, commanded by General Winfield S. Hancock, arrived that evening, but no attack was launched to further Federal gains.

On June 16, a series of unimaginative piecemeal attacks was launched with little coordination between the two Union corps on the field. Every single attack was repulsed by Beauregard's men. On June 17, Federal efforts were reinforced, prompting localized progress, but still they were unable to seize victory. The following day was expected to bring the grand success Grant planned for when he decided to shift his army in this direction. Time was beginning to run out though. General Robert E. Lee was becoming suspicious of the affairs in his front. Federal hopes were pinned to the following day's results.

Throughout the afternoon of June 17, the 21st Pennsylvania Cavalry, with the rest of the brigade, shifted southwest and extended the Union line beyond Burnside's Ninth Corps toward the Norfolk and Petersburg Railroad. "We marched over the field where the second Corps had been engaged the day before, and the ground was covered with their dead," wrote a member of the regiment. After halting, the men took a rest and were joined by two new veteran regiments to the brigade, the 91st and 155th Pennsylvania. This made up for the loss of the 9th Massachusetts, which mustered out of service the week before. Still, the 21st Pennsylvania remained the largest regiment in the brigade. After their performance at Cold Harbor, it seems the veteran units were well satisfied with these dismounted cavalrymen.[146]

Everyone in the regiment had learned well that the opportunity for rest was ever-fleeting. Major Bell wrote to his wife, "The Ball as it is called is commencing in earnest and it is expected that there will be desperate fighting this evening about six PM, as we must have Petersburg." As it turned out, there was no fighting for the 21st that evening, but orders were issued for an assault at four o'clock the following morning. Only a few hundred yards away in the so-called Hagood Line, General Beauregard ordered his men to quietly withdraw under the cover of darkness to a more consolidated line of fortifications, backing ever closer to the city of Petersburg.[147]

Sweitzer's brigade, a small piece of the nine full Union divisions making preparations, assembled for its assault at the appointed staging area and time on the morning of June 18. Then the men advanced over an open space, expecting the shots to ring out at any moment. Much to their surprise, there was no resistance at all. Confused, Union officers dispatched riders up and down the line trying to ascertain what was going on. Then they pressed skirmishers forward to locate where the Southerners had gone. The 62nd Pennsylvania and 22nd Massachusetts were sent on to the skirmish line under the command of Colonel William Tilton and advanced through a deep cut created years before by the construction of the Norfolk and Petersburg Railroad. There they found the enemy and called up support.[148]

Colonel Sweitzer held the remaining regiments at the ready, and they "kept up a brisk fire." However, it was not until about noon that the 21st Pennsylvania Cavalry, under the command of Lieutenant Colonel Moson, finally advanced with the balance of the brigade. Difficulties from topography made communications and coordination challenging. Brigade commanders could not keep track of the movements on their flanks. This caused units to become separated and fight independently of one another.

All the while, more and more Confederate reinforcements were shuttling toward the Petersburg defenses. General Robert E. Lee finally knew with certainty the new Union objective. The delay on the part of the Federals, coupled with their tentative attack, sank their now quickly fading opportunity for a swift and decisive victory at Petersburg.

The 21st Pennsylvania Cavalry advanced a short distance with bayonets fixed "on a yell" over the brow of a hill before descending into a ravine along the banks of Poor (or Taylor's) Creek, directly below the enemy's new line of defenses. The men were greeted with a volley of musketry from the earthworks in their front and

Commissary Sergeant Edward Heckman, from Pine Grove in Schuylkill County, was wounded at Petersburg on June 18. *Author's collection.*

Marion H. Baker of Company E was wounded on June 18 and died eight days later at City Point. *Author's collection.*

above them. "We charged through a hailstorm of grape & canister," reported Private Samuel Glass. At least sixteen pieces of enemy artillery were trained in their direction. The regimental colors went down at least four times but were raised aloft again each time. As one man recalled, "If Cold Harbor was hard, the fight of the 18th of June was harder."[149]

Company B was hit particularly hard. Lieutenant Henry G. Lott of Gettysburg was shot in the head and barely clung to life as he was shuttled rearward. Also of Company B, twenty-six-year-old carpenter Lafayette Brenizer of Arendtsville was dangerously shot in the neck. Private Conrad Linn was shot through both legs. Lieutenant Colonel Moson was hit in the hand but remained on the field trying to steady the men. Major Charles F. Gillies was thrust into regimental command, but his battlefield promotion was short-lived. Down he went as well, shot in the leg.[150]

Making it to within about 150 yards of the enemy works, the 21st was pinned down with little room to maneuver. The combat settled into a sporadic, haphazard firefight. Men continued to fall. Frank Neil of Company M was shot through the right leg. He was one of the lucky men to be carried rearward, although it was quickly determined that amputation was the only course of action. The procedure was completed efficiently, but the young man never recovered. He died the following day, only sixteen years old.

The 21st Pennsylvania pulled back from its advanced position about twenty-five yards to a less exposed piece of ground. "Some carried rails and built works, others kept up a heavy fire on the fort, which effectually silenced their artillery." The men remained under fire until the following morning when they were relieved. Elsewhere along the Federal lines, more bloody attacks were made through the evening of June 18, but all failed to drive the Confederates from their strong position.[151]

Another attempt was made four days later to force the Confederates out of their earthworks. The 21st Pennsylvania with the rest of Sweitzer's brigade was moved to the left of the army's line near the Jerusalem Plank Road in support of the Second Corps, which was attempting to flank the enemy out of their Petersburg positions. This, too, failed and drove up casualties severely on the Federal side. If Grant wanted to invest Petersburg, he would have to try another way. As Major Bell put it, "[A]s fast as we move they move and from present indications it will land both armies down about the Gulf of Mexico next, each one throwing up entrenchments as they go along."

In the ranks of the 21st Pennsylvania Cavalry, news poured in from various hospitals about the condition of officers and men. About one hundred men were killed, wounded or still missing. At least nineteen men were killed or

Lieutenant Henry G. Lott of Adams County received a head wound on June 18 at Petersburg that proved mortal. *Author's collection.*

eventually died from their wounds on June 18. Another four died of wounds received on June 22. Major Gillies's right leg was amputated above the knee. It was expected that Lieutenant Colonel Moson would lose his left hand. Due to attrition in the regiment, Major Oliver B. Knowles, who was then serving as a staff officer, was relieved from that duty to return to the regiment and take command.

Lieutenant Henry G. Lott of Adams County was given a favorable prospect by the regimental surgeon. The young man was eventually transported to a hospital in Annapolis, Maryland, but there he succumbed to his wound on June 28. His remains were transported to Gettysburg. He was interred at Evergreen Cemetery on Cemetery Hill two days later, overlooking the site where his comrade George W. Sandoe became the company's first death one year before. A five-stanza poem was written to honor Lieutenant Lott's sacrifice by an unknown source in Franklin County, quite possibly one of his former men: "His comrades may be watching, From dark till early dawn, For their brother soldier who will never more return. No more will earthly troubles Disturb his peaceful rest, For now he is reposing Upon the Saviour's breast."

The regiment next made several short moves along the line but was spared any direct action for a while. Lucky as it was, the temperatures were oppressive, ranging up toward one hundred degrees during the day. Adding to the discomfort, no precipitation had fallen during the previous weeks, and the ground was covered in a powdery dust that was about six inches deep. During the hottest part of the day, the landscape transformed into a virtual desert as the soft breeze lifted the dust, decreasing visibility at times to fifty yards. Enshrouded in this inhospitable environment as the men were, reality sunk in that the only way to victory at Petersburg was by siege.[152]

The men settled in along the army's center, and slowly the days ticked by as they played their part in this new style of siege warfare. In early July, this relegated them to fatigue duty for almost two weeks, constructing earthworks, digging trenches and improving army roadways. It was monotonous and hard work, but the alternative was no more inviting.

The dangers were still ubiquitous. Lieutenant Benjamin J. Levy, in charge of commissary for the regiment, and Captain Albert T. Clark of Company M shared a tent together. One night while fast asleep, a solid shot "came crashing through the back of the tent, struck between them, ricochetted, and killed an inoffensive mule." A narrow escape it was for the two officers, though not for the mule.

On July 13, the regiment relieved the 155th Pennsylvania on the front line of works and remained there for eight days. After this stint, it again removed to the rear and continued its manual labor. During this time, some of the men who had been convalescing from previous wounds began to return to the regiment, including Lieutenant Martin P. Doyle. Of Doyle it was written, "In the field he is represented as the fearless, brave, intrepid officer, the idol of his men and superiors; and whose moral courage is only equalled by his desire to crush the rebellion, and crush it quickly." With all the battlefield losses to the regiment's officer corps, returns like Doyle's were important. Much of July passed without any more major combat, but not without its share of tumult.[153]

Confederate brigadier general John McCausland led nearly three thousand Confederate horsemen into Pennsylvania seeking revenge for the atrocities committed by Union general David Hunter's forces operating in the Shenandoah Valley. The Southern force arrived in Chambersburg on July 30, demanding an impossible ransom of the citizenry with the threat of burning the town to the ground. The demand being unsatisfied, McCausland's men torched the community. In the process they destroyed nearly five hundred structures, which left about two thousand civilians homeless.[154]

One house that managed to escape the flames that day stood northwest of the town on an eminence known as Federal Hill. Confederate colonel Harry Gilmor wrote in his postwar memoir that he and two men approached the fine brick house and informed the woman residing there that they must "perform the extremely unpleasant duty of burning her house." Breakfast sat on the table, and the woman invited the enemy soldiers to partake while she gathered some items of personal value. Upon finishing breakfast, the woman began to converse with Gilmor, and he inquired after her husband's name. "Colonel Boyd, of the Union Army" was her response, at which the colonel gasped in disbelief. He told Mrs. Boyd, "I knew her husband, and had fought against him for two years in the Valley of Virginia; that he had gained a high reputation among the citizens for kindness and gentlemanly conduct; that while we were there for the purpose of punishing vandalism, we were ready and anxious to repay acts of kindness done to our people….I told her that her house should not be burned."[155]

Burned-out ruins of downtown Chambersburg. This image was taken by Chambersburg photographer Henry Bishop, and copies were "sold for the benefit of the sufferers." *Author's collection.*

The colonel himself was away from Chambersburg on account of his wounds. His right arm was paralyzed, and numerous doctors in Philadelphia and New York were consulted about extracting the ball from near his spine. The concern was the projectile's proximity to the carotid artery in his right neck. Still, in this condition he reported for duty and took up a small command in Hagerstown, Maryland, upon the withdrawal of enemy forces by August 7. With each examination of the wound, it was becoming more plainly evident that the colonel's options for returning to the field were diminishing.[156]

The news of Chambersburg shocked the Union and exacerbated fears of another major Confederate thrust into Pennsylvania. This, of course, quickly proved to be unfounded. There were mixed reactions across the Confederacy, although some felt the event did more to hurt the Southern cause than help. "As if to stimulate the tardy Pennsylvanians to rush to arms against us," wrote a correspondent of the *Charleston Mercury*, "Chambersburg is burned down." This South Carolinian may well have been on to something, as there was an uptick in Pennsylvania's enlistments after the event, although it is impossible to discern individual motivations on such a broad scale. One thing is certain, however. Discontent and anger over the event definitely extended into the ranks of the 21st Pennsylvania.[157]

On the day Chambersburg burned, the regiment witnessed the explosion of Burnside's mine constructed by their fellow Pennsylvanians over the previous weeks. Though not directly engaged, the men had quite a vantage. While observing developments from atop his bombproof, "one of the bravest and best officers," Captain John H. Harmony of Company L, was hit in the arm by a spent bullet. His time in the army was not yet concluded though. After the disaster that became known as "The Crater" and learning of what transpired at Chambersburg, Major Bell could only muster, "Oh but it is discouraging."[158]

The immediate situation for the regiment remained relatively docile through the early part of August, but on August 15, the division was replaced by the Ninth Corps on the front line. The 21st Pennsylvania Cavalry was placed in reserve "with orders to be ready to move at a moment's notice." On the morning of August 18, the regiment began marching toward the army's left. It covered about five miles along the Jerusalem Plank Road. "We soon passed the advance cavalry picket, then under cover of a friendly ridge," wrote Lieutenant Doyle, "and formed in three lines of battle. We deployed skirmishers and drove in the enemy's pickets, and we advancing through swamps of mud and water knee deep, soon reached the railroad after capturing some twenty Rebels." The railroad Doyle spoke of was the Weldon Railroad, a vital supply link that ran south from Petersburg to Weldon and, eventually, the Confederacy's only remaining port, Wilmington, North Carolina.

Major Knowles ordered the regiment to commence destroying the tracks and telegraph wires. "The regiment pitched into the work with great avidity, exclaiming as they capsized the track, 'Remember Chambersburg!'" Several miles of track were wrecked, but because of their proximity to the enemy and now on the army's left flank, it was determined to prepare for the enemy. Hasty breastworks were constructed—and just in time too.

At about noon, a rainstorm washed out the landscape, and it was closely followed by a Confederate attack led by Major General Henry Heth. "After our men poured several volleys into them, we in return charged on them driving them." The conflict swayed back and forth around the rail line for several hours, with the Federals surrendering the most ground, although they still held the important railroad line. As Lieutenant Doyle keenly asserted, "The enemy is in earnest, trying to regain this road; and from their furious and numerous charges we are led to believe that their very existence depends on the possession of this road."[159]

The men of the 21st kept to strengthening their position over the next several days. More Confederate attacks were launched, but by August 21, the Army of the Potomac still held the important railroad. Another of the 21st Pennsylvania's line officers fell on the last day of fighting at the Weldon Railroad. First Lieutenant James Speer Orr of Johnstown, only twenty-three years old, died of his wounds on August 22. The regiment lost two more men killed, Privates Hugh Deihl and Milton Naugle, both of Company G. Another ten were wounded, some of the more than six thousand casualties in the three days of fighting. Though at a great cost, another lifeline for Robert E. Lee's army was permanently severed, and the resource-starved Army of Northern Virginia was a step closer to its demise. On August 27, the regiment was pulled off the front line. Much of September passed largely without incident beyond the doldrums of digging, at least on the Virginia front.[160]

Nearly three hundred miles away at Pottsville, Pennsylvania, the situation among civilians was insatiable. Riots were intermittently popping up throughout Schuylkill County and at other locations throughout the state, usually ignited by antiwar Democrats. In some instances, the troops sent to patrol these neighborhoods found themselves caught in the discord. Such was the case on September 17, 1864.

The group Democracy of Schuylkill County held its largest ever gathering at Pottsville that day, and by all accounts it was peaceful. One newspaper correspondent mentioned, "They met without arms in their hands, not dreaming of insult and outrage." An immense crowd had filled the streets and neighborhood for four hours and at the conclusion of the meeting began to disperse. It was in these moments that "a party of twenty cavalrymen, with drawn sabres, rushed out of a by street, and attacked the people." These men belonged to Captain Josiah C. Hullinger's Company D of the 21st Pennsylvania.

It is unknown who ordered this action or if any officers were even present. Nor is it known whether or not the event simply unfolded in the spur of the moment. Regardless, the scene was ugly. The troopers went through the crowd "cutting and slashing" with their sabers, and when the civilians realized what was happening, "they turned on the soldiers and began hurling stones and clubs at them." Realizing that the situation was not in their favor, the members of Company D quickly cut their way through the crowd and escaped.

Six civilians were wounded. One of them was a Union veteran who had just returned home after serving more than three years. That evening, the organization publicly denounced the affair and determined it best for Democrats attending the succeeding events to come armed. Of course, opposing political parties blamed the constituents of their counterparts for inciting the violence. These violent occurrences would become more frequent as the country moved toward the fall elections, which only served to escalate tensions about which direction the country would go.[161]

Back in Virginia, the Fifth Corps was reorganized, and the 21st Pennsylvania Cavalry (dismounted) found itself brigaded on September 24 with Colonel Horatio G. Sickel's brand-new 198th Pennsylvania Volunteer Infantry, which formed in Philadelphia during the previous two weeks. Although the men of the 21st could not boast of an extensive fighting record, they were definitely experienced next to the 198th

CDV of an unknown trooper, likely of Company D of the 21st Pennsylvania Cavalry, taken at Scranton. *Author's collection.*

and surely skeptical of how their new brigade mates might react in the heat of battle.[162]

Six days later, on September 30, the new brigade moved into action, marching westward along the Poplar Springs Road as part of a larger operation by Grant to get at Lee's flanks. Really the day's move on the west end of the line was meant only to be a demonstration, to keep Confederate forces from reinforcing their left and the operations of Yankees on the opposite end of the line. The brigade advanced steadily until being ordered to lie down in a belt of woods. There the men lay for some time under the enemy's screeching shells that did little damage. Finally, the brigade was ordered to advance, but the 198th misunderstood its orders. The 21st Pennsylvania charged with its old brigade mates on this day, commanded by Colonel Edgar M. Gregory, although its left flank was precariously exposed.

Realizing the mistake, Colonel Sickel's brigade adjutant general, Captain John E. Parsons, personally led the 198th Pennsylvania out to the left to its assigned position just as the wave of blue crossed the Squirrel Level Road toward Peebles Farm. The enemy troops to their front

The Battle of Peeble's Farm, as published in *Frank Leslie's Illustrated Newspaper. Author's collection.*

belonged to the division commanded by General Robert E. Lee's son W.H.F. "Rooney" Lee. Although they fought doggedly, the Yankee attack overran the Confederate earthworks, driving enemy troops back toward the Boydton Plank Road, gate to the South Side Railroad and one of the few remaining options connecting Robert E. Lee's Confederate army with the outside world.[163]

Fifth Corps commander General G.K. Warren proudly boasted that very night, "The Fifth Corps has done splendidly today; principally Griffin," which included the 21st Pennsylvania Cavalry. Private David Miller of Company L was the only man of the regiment killed outright in the fight on September 30. His remains were taken home to Marion in Franklin County, where the twenty-four-year-old was laid to rest at the Salem Evangelical Lutheran Church. Nine others were wounded in what became known as the Battle of Peebles Farm or Poplar Spring Church. Among them, William H. Hutchison (only two days a corporal) of Company I succumbed to his wounds on October 24. Private James W. Hoover of Company C had to have his right arm cut off. In a world where the thread between those who lived and died seemed so tenuous, Hoover defied time, living until 1909.

The regiment remained in position that night, strengthening the earthworks and bracing for the moment all knew was ahead: another push westward to seal off the enemy's escape routes. There were also rumors circulating about the uncertain future that kept many men curious.

The presidential election was a little more than a month away, and the outcome of the war hung in the balance, very much dependent on the results. Regardless of all the unanswered questions, the men of the Army of the Potomac were one step closer to an end of some kind, and the 21st Pennsylvania Cavalry would be there to see it through.[164]

Chapter 10

ANY AMOUNT OF THE JONIES

Remounted and the Winter of 1864–65

Only one day after the battle at Peebles Farm, the 21st Pennsylvania Cavalry was ordered away from the front and began a march toward City Point. It was headed for Giesboro, just south of Washington, D.C., the Union army's large central remount camp. After nearly five months serving as infantry in the Army of the Potomac, the boys of the 21st were getting their horses and accoutrements back to join the cavalry corps.

A man in the ranks believed it was "done at the suggestion of the division and corps Generals as a compliment for the gallant behavior of the regiment in the recent battles before Petersburg." Their brigade commander of but a short time, Colonel Horatio Sickel, wrote to Major Knowles, "I feel it but justice to you and the brave men under your command to bear testimony to their courage, valor and gallantry in the late battles near Poplar Grove Church, and while I regret the loss of the regiment from the brigade, I regard the remounting of the regiment at this time but a fitting reward and acknowledgement of their continued good services, while temporarily serving as infantry." Sickel closed his letter well understanding the road ahead: "I assure you that in [the] future I will watch with deep interest for the deeds of valor which I well know will be enacted by them on other battlefields."[165]

There may have been some truth to being rewarded for good service, but more reasonably, the Army of the Potomac was sorely missing cavalry because Major General Phil Sheridan had the majority of the mounted arm on campaign up the Shenandoah Valley. The cavalry still at Petersburg were further diminished from raids into enemy territory that sapped the available force. Only one of the Army of the Potomac's cavalry divisions under the capable and experienced leadership of Brigadier General David M. Gregg remained at Petersburg.

The boys of the 21st Pennsylvania were "in high glee over the event"; as a newspaper correspondent confidently suggested, "They will no doubt prove as efficient and gallant mounted as they have on foot." It took two weeks to get the entire regiment fitted with horses. Sergeant Isaac N.S. Wile of Company I wrote home that by "the 18th ult., our regiment was once more seen in line, fully equipped as cavalry and on good horses." Little time was wasted getting the regiment back to the front.[166]

John A. Holman from Mexico, Juniata County, was a member of Company C. *Author's collection.*

Major Oliver B. Knowles led the regiment back to the Weldon Railroad. It was ordered to join the Third Brigade of the Second Cavalry Division commanded by Colonel Charles H. Smith, which included two veteran units tried and true: the 1st Maine and 6th Ohio Cavalry.[167]

While the 21st was refitting, General Grant played host to Secretary of War Edwin Stanton. The party toured the siege lines at Petersburg to explore opportunities to break the stalemate. Stanton implored Grant to hold out on any further operations, believing that failure would ruin chances for success at the polls in November. Certainly, in other theaters there was much to be impressed by. The key city of Atlanta fell to Sherman's army in July. A short time after the secretary of war's visit to Petersburg, General Phil Sheridan defeated the Confederate force under Jubal Early in the Shenandoah Valley, snatching victory from defeat at the Battle of Cedar Creek. However, it was clear that weariness about the Petersburg front was sinking public confidence.

Despite Stanton's advice, Grant believed that success at Petersburg could sway voters to the Republican cause of prosecuting the war to a successful conclusion. On the advice of Army of the Potomac commander Major General George G. Meade, Grant decided to make another attempt against the South Side Railroad and outflank Lee's right flank. The army's sixth offensive at Petersburg was born on October 24 with orders from Grant to Meade stating, "Make preparations to march out at an early hour on the 27th to gain possession of the South Side Railroad, and to hold it and fortify it back to your present left. In commencing your advance, move in three columns." Of course, General Gregg's cavalry, almost all of them, would play an important role if the plans were to be executed successfully.[168]

Details for the move were spelled out the following day. General Gregg's cavalry was to move as part of General Winfield S. Hancock's Second Corps:

> *General Gregg will concentrate his cavalry on the afternoon of the 26th instant* [Wednesday] *at some point toward the left convenient for crossing Hatcher's Run by the first route below that used by Hancock's infantry, and which shall not disclose the movement to the observation of the enemy. Every precaution will be taken to conceal the movement. His pickets from the vicinity of the plank road westward will be relieved in time to accompany him on the morning of the 27th. Upon concentrating his command he will report to Major-General Hancock. General Gregg will move on the morning of the 27th (Thursday), not later than 2 o'clock, cross Hatcher's Run below the Second Corps and move on the left of the infantry, probably using the Quaker road as far as the Boydton plank. His route must be governed by that of the Second Corps.*

Gregg was given even more particulars by Hancock, being told to move by the Rowanty Post Office to the Vaughan Road.[169]

General Gregg then disseminated particulars to his three brigades. The 21st Pennsylvania Cavalry, with the rest of the Third Brigade, was ordered to concentrate with the division near Perkins House and prepare four days' rations for the impending movement. Gregg explicitly ordered no calls to be sounded until further orders in an effort to keep movements concealed.[170]

When morning finally came, Colonel Charles H. Smith's brigade, including the 21st Pennsylvania Cavalry, led the way. It was before 4:00 a.m. All the cavalry's movements on the day would be dictated by what happened to Hancock's Second Corps. Gregg's division took "the road leading from the Weldon railroad by Rowanty Post-Office (Billups P.O.) to the crossing of the Rowanty below Arthur's Swamp, thence across to the Quaker road, and following this to the (Boydton) plank road."

Before reaching the Quaker Road, the column first encountered the enemy at the Hargrave farm, east of the Rowanty Creek. The enemy was behind breastworks, and Smith quickly dismounted parts of the 1st

Maine and 6th Ohio, with the balance and the 21st Pennsylvania Cavalry in support. The order to advance came swiftly and there was little contest, with the Confederates fleeing across the stream. Several of them were captured and provided intelligence that General Rooney Lee's division of Confederate cavalry was encamped only about three miles to the column's left (or south) near Stony Creek. General Matthew Butler's division was directly to the right-front up the Quaker Road, blocking their path to the Boydton Plank Road.[171]

Shortly after reaching the confluence of Hatcher's Run and Gravelly Run, the Yankee column turned right and trotted up the Quaker Road. There the enemy was posted in force:

> *The enemy's position was one of great natural strength. Upon a commanding eminence was a section of artillery, which, upon the appearance of the head of my column, opened fire. A strong line of skirmishers was displayed. The Sixth Ohio and First Maine were dismounted, and, as skirmishers, waded the creek, and, assisted by the Twenty-first Pennsylvania (mounted), attacked the enemy's line. This line, resisting strongly, was forced back beyond the heights, and then discovering the advance of the Second Army Corps on the right, fled in great haste in a southerly direction.*

Major Knowles's Pennsylvanians impressed their veteran brigade mates. During the crossing, the regiment split in half, and each half moved to extend either flank in the charge, thus outflanking the enemy works. Finally closing the gap with the advancing Second Corps on their right also offered some security.[172]

The division pushed northward up the Quaker Road, conforming to the movements of the infantry. Finally, the men reached the Boydton Plank Road, where Gregg deployed Kerwin's Second Brigade on the west side of the intersection. Smith's Third Brigade was deployed across the Boydton Plank Road fronting southward. Davies's First Brigade was positioned fronting to the southeast toward the direction from which it had just traveled, straddling the Quaker Road. The hope now was for Hancock's infantry to get to the White Oak Road and move toward the Southside Railroad. However, it was not to be on this day.

Confederate troops under the command of Major General Henry Heth discovered the plot and moved to strike the Second Corps in the vicinity of Burgess Mill, where Hatcher's Run crossed the Boydton Plank Road just to the north of the White Oak Road. Confederate cavalry under Butler fought

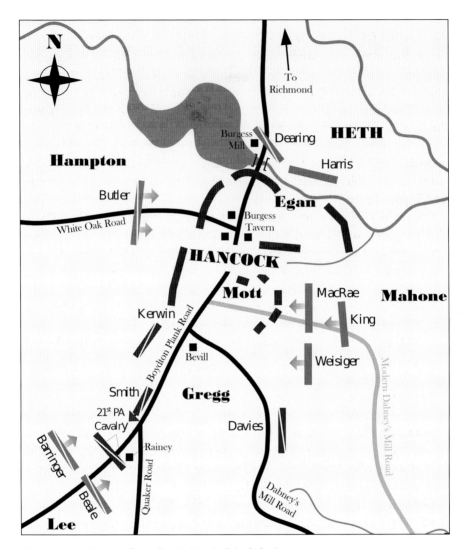

The Battle of Boydton Plank Road. *Map by Britt C. Isenberg.*

stubbornly to hang on until the gray infantry could arrive. General Gregg was forced to dismount much of his division to support the infantry. This left the 21st Pennsylvania Cavalry alone astride the Boydton Plank Road, the most southern Federal regiment on the battlefield. It could clearly hear the din of battle raging to the north as successive regiments from either side joined the tilt, although things were ominously quiet on its front.

Suddenly, the air around the men was broken by hissing shells from four Confederate cannons of McGregor's Battery, part of Rooney Lee's cavalry division, which had just arrived south of the 21st Pennsylvania Cavalry along the planked roadway. Private Samuel Glass related to his wife that they found "any amount of the Jo[h]nies." Major Knowles ordered most of the men to dismount. The shells came quicker, but the regiment had to stand alone for some time, "gallantly and persistently" resisting the attack. There were moments when the fighting closed to a hand-to-hand encounter, but the 21st "maintained its ground till the rest of the brigade…could be withdrawn and brought up as re-enforcements." The Confederate regiment that took the worst of this charge was the veteran 9th Virginia Cavalry.[173]

It was likely in this close encounter when Lieutenant William Chandler of Company G was wounded and taken prisoner. Chandler was one of those line officers who held the deepest confidence of the men he commanded. Only seven days prior, he was honored at a presentation ceremony near City Point. His men presented him with "a beautiful saddle and horse equipments and sabre and belt." Sergeant James T. Rogers spoke on behalf of the men, saying, "He has been to us all that we could expect or ask of any one—who has nobly stood by us, whether in camp, or on the march, or facing the iron hail of rebel soldiery." Chandler was sent to Richmond, where he began a stint at the infamous Libby Prison.[174]

Company I's Sergeant Isaac N.S. Will of Lancaster remembered being outnumbered three to one and taking fire from three different directions. His captain, Elias McMellen, who was then commanding the second battalion, took a bullet through the thigh while trying to rally his men. Also wounded for the second time that year was Lieutenant Martin P. Doyle. Both officers were safely evacuated from the field.[175]

General Gregg witnessed the stand of the division's newest regiment, the 21st Pennsylvania Cavalry, and admired its pluck, saying in his official report that the men "stoutly" resisted the enemy's attacks and could not be beaten back "save inch by inch." Finally arriving on the scene, the 1st Maine Cavalry joined the 21st Pennsylvania's right's flank. Eventually, the 6th Ohio came up to extend the line even farther to the right in a semicircle. The troopers were supported by Reynolds's Battery I, 1st U.S. Artillery. The fighting continued to swirl along the roadway, but both sides stuck to their positions at a distance. Meanwhile, behind them to the north a massive Confederate counterattack dislodged several Second Corps positions, which now made Gregg's troopers vulnerable in the rear. The good news was that General Hancock dispatched Kerwin's brigade down the roadway to the support of Smith.[176]

The sun was setting on a long day when Gregg ordered his division to retrace the route of its morning advance in reverse. The men were hampered at Gravelly Run since Gregg ordered his men to destroy it after crossing earlier that day. The troopers did not arrive back at Perkins House until about seven o'clock on the morning of October 28.[177]

The 21st Pennsylvania Cavalry's first battle with Gregg's division was no skirmish. The regiment lost eight men killed or died of wounds, thirty-two wounded (four of whom were captured) and three who were wounded and never found. Among the forty-three casualties were seven line officers.

General Gregg complimented the entire brigade in its first battle with the words, "My entire command behaved

Lieutenant John T. Pfoutz of Company L was wounded at the Boydton Plank Road on October 27, 1864. *Author's collection.*

with great gallantry." Surely the veterans of the 1st Maine and 6th Ohio were skeptical of the abilities of the 21st when they rode out of camp before sunrise on October 27, and they had every right to be. The regimental historian of the 1st Maine Cavalry may have paid the 21st Pennsylvania its greatest compliment, however subtly, for the fight at Boydton Plank Road: "The First Maine boys became acquainted with the fighting qualities of the new regiments with which they were brigaded: the men of the new regiments became acquainted, by observation, with the First Maine, and there was confidence throughout the brigade."[178]

The offensive to cut the Southside Railroad was a failure. The 21st Pennsylvania Cavalry acquitted itself well and proved the decision to remount the regiment a good one. For many in the ranks, the most important victory was still ahead—although it was not on the field of battle, it certainly would determine the fate of their cause. As Sergeant Isaac N.S. Will put it, "The victory which we will achieve by ballot on the 8th will prove more disastrous to the rebels than any victory ever won by the sword. Their last hope will be blasted. They will find the election of McClellan, and not the war, a failure. The best use they can make of their navy is to fit out their boats for a trip up Salt River with 'the Little Napoleon' for commander."[179]

Even if Will's hyperbole never came to fruition, President Lincoln did win a second term, and the war would continue to an end. In the 21st Pennsylvania Cavalry, 244 votes went to Lincoln and 106 to McClellan. It was also during that week that the men learned Colonel Boyd would not return to command on account of his wounds. He was formally discharged from the service of the United States.

Regardless of major political happenings and personal disappointments, the mission of the cavalry continued unabated, and rumors were swirling. The day before the election, the regiment moved with the rest of the brigade on a scout down the Weldon Railroad six miles beyond Ream's Station to Stony Creek. General Gregg learned that the enemy planned on building a branch line from the Weldon Railroad at Stony Creek to the Southside Railroad, reestablishing a continuous rail line into Petersburg. This reconnaissance mission provided the information that spawned a far more robust operation ahead.[180]

On December 7, the 21st Pennsylvania Cavalry moved with the rest of the division and a portion of General Warren's Fifth Corps with the purpose of destroying more distant sections of the Weldon Railroad. It was known that the enemy was using the railroad up to Stony Creek and then transporting supplies via wagon to Petersburg for Lee's army.

The Federal horsemen led the infantry and crossed the Nottoway River at Freeman's Bridge. Then they passed through Sussex Court House and bivouacked for the night. Smith's Third Brigade debarked from bivouac with the objective of destroying the Nottoway railroad bridge on the morning of the eighth. As General Gregg related in his report, "This was speedily accomplished, the enemy having fled upon our approach."

The troopers pressed on toward Jarratt's Station. The trailing brigade, commanded by Brigadier General J. Irvin Gregg, was attacked on the Halifax Road but was driven back to the Nottoway River by Major Alender P. Duncan's 4th Pennsylvania Cavalry. The command continued down the Halifax Road, followed by Fifth Corps infantry, and started destroying a one-mile section of the Weldon Railroad. All their efforts were turned to ruining the track until evening was upon them. "As fast as the road was torn up the ties were piled up and fired, and the rails placed on top in order to bend them and render them unfit for future use. Not a single tie or rail was left." Their hard work finished, at Jarratt's Station they bivouacked for the night. Gregg and Warren held conference that evening, and it was decided that the expedition would head for home at daylight.

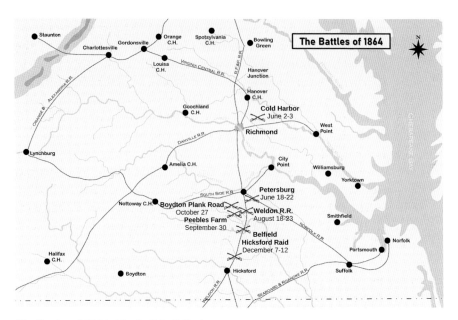

The Battles of 1864. *Map by Britt C. Isenberg.*

Smith's brigade was chosen to serve as the rearguard for the entire column, with the honors going to the 21st Pennsylvania Cavalry. To provide plenty of room for other units to vacate the area, Smith's men moved to Belfield near Hicksford and went back to work destroying railroad from there back to Three Creeks. Meanwhile, the Fifth Corps infantry was marching north as was a portion of Gregg's division.[181]

On the frigid morning of December 10, Smith's brigade finally began its return to base as the snow fell around the men. Shortly after starting out, Confederate cavalry attacked. It was a running fight, but the 21st kept them at bay for a stretch of approximately three to four miles. The troops were supported by portions of the 1st Maine Cavalry and Dennison's Horse Battery A of the 2nd U.S. Artillery. Major Bell told his wife that he and his comrades "gave them thunder." They received plenty also. Major Richard Ryckman's horse was killed under him by a Confederate shell, but he escaped on foot.

Near Three Creeks, four companies of the 21st were drawn up in line of battle near a house on the south side of the creek. "As soon as the rebels came in view," remembered Bell, "firing on both sides commenced and as the house was only frame, the Rebel bullets went crashing through it." There was a woman with her four children inside. She came running to the door screaming with the two youngest in her arms. Major Bell yelled for her to get into the basement for safety. In a few moments, the men of the 21st were ordered back across the stream "to give our artillery a chance to play on the Rebels." Dennison's battery had little margin for error with the lines so close. Bell and his men were "not fifty yards down the hill from the house till crash went one of our shells" right through the house.

The men of the 21st got across the bridge and tore it up to slow the Southerners. Of course, this also brought the Confederate line up to the poor woman's house, which overlooked the stream. "Our battery commenced raining shells and canister in and around it and in less time than it takes to tell it the flames burst out from the roof and what became of that poor woman and children I cannot tell for she would have to run the gauntlet of fire from 500 carbines as well as from our battery."

Slowly, realizing they were outnumbered, the Confederate pursuers called off the chase. The action was brief but severe. Three men of the 21st Pennsylvania Cavalry were killed or died of wounds, six were wounded and one was missing. The rearguard cautiously withdrew with the snow getting deeper by the hour. General Gregg seemed pleased by the effort, writing, "[A] well organized rear…was more than enough to prevent any advantage to the enemy."

The expedition tore up nearly twenty miles of track during the trek toward the North Carolina border and thwarted, at least for a time, any immediate possibility of building a branch line to alleviate besieged Confederate troops at Petersburg. It also appears that the column did more in the way of destruction than only laying waste to the railroad, although this was, not surprisingly, omitted from any official reports. "I saw more on this last raid down to Hicksford than I ever wish to see again of the effects of this cruel and merciless war," wrote Major Robert Bell. "Grandmothers, wives and children driven out of their houses at all hours of the night among

Sergeant William F. Selser of Company L from Mercersburg in Franklin County. *Author's collection.*

thousands of soldiers and their houses fired before they had left the doors and often not a thing around their shivering forms but what they had on them and no shelter provably for ten miles as every house, barn, out house with reach destroyed. Our line of march was literally lit up one whole night be the conflagrations and some of the houses were most splendid residences." Difficult as witnessing these events must have been for individual soldiers, the only solace was in believing that these actions were a means to the end of the war.[182]

Chapter 11

THE RECALL WAS SOUNDED

The Last Campaign

Whether or not the Union men in the siege lines at Petersburg truly understood the gravity of unfolding events, the war was rapidly shifting to a conclusion. At Nashville, General George H. Thomas, the "Rock of Chickamauga," defeated Confederate general John Bell Hood's Army of the Tennessee once and for all. On December 21, 1864, the commander who defeated Hood at Atlanta the previous summer, General William Tecumseh Sherman, completed his March to the Sea and captured the city of Savannah, Georgia. The expedition was an arrow that pierced the heart of the Confederacy. Even Lee's veterans at Petersburg were running out of time with ever-withering arteries of supply.

After the successful raid to Belfield, weather led to a cessation of any major operations through the holiday season. Both armies built winter quarters, and the monotony of camp life once again settled across the lines. Despite the occasional rotation to the front line, which brought men under fire, the winter largely dawned a momentary respite from all the previous month's tribulations. There was no doubt in anyone's mind, however, that the reprieve was only temporary.

There was plenty of time for soldiers to reflect on their own well-being and the general state of affairs. Private Harry W. Blakemore of Company M wrote to his cousin from the cavalry hospital at City Point, "When I was captured my horse run away with every thing I owned so I was left of a desolate character and that I have got pretty used to it by this time for I have been left so quite a number of times now." Still, he and his comrades persevered.[183]

Many officers in the regiment applied for leaves of absence to visit loved ones. In some cases, loved ones came to them—or, at the very least, they would find opportune times to visit friends and family serving in other units within the army and in proximity. On January 16, 1865, Major Robert Bell and Captain James Mickley took the time to revisit the scene of the fighting the previous June to see the spot where their friend Lieutenant Henry G. Lott was mortally wounded. "It seems so strange that the town [Petersburg] lies in plain view since the timber has been cut down," wrote Major Bell, "and we cannot go in."[184]

The year 1865 began with a command shuffle largely due to attrition. Major Oliver B. Knowles was promoted to colonel and temporarily commanded the Third Brigade since Colonel Smith was on leave. Major Bell commanded the regiment. Company D was finally relieved from the duty of assisting civil authorities in northeastern Pennsylvania to rejoin the regiment at Petersburg. Company E was detached from the regiment to serve with Sixth Corps headquarters, where it would remain through February.[185]

At 3:00 a.m. on the morning of February 5, Colonel Knowles led the Third Brigade out of camp to Gary's Church, Ream's Station and eventually Dinwiddie Court House before turning back toward Rowanty as part of a larger operation. The objective for Gregg's cavalry division was to intercept Confederate supply wagons utilizing the Boydton Plank Road with the support of General Warren's Fifth Corps.

The brigade began marching again shortly after midnight on February 6 to the Vaughan Road in support of Warren's infantry along Hatcher's Run who were attacked by Confederates under Major General John B. Gordon. The only regiment of the brigade that saw significant action that day was the 6th Ohio Cavalry. The 21st Pennsylvania Cavalry was split up, with half ordered to report to General Samuel Crawford of the Fifth Corps and the other half sent with a staff officer of army commander General George G. Meade.

The brigade returned to the Weldon Railroad on February 7 and then back to its camp the following day. In the end, the operation was unsuccessful. The 21st Pennsylvania escaped with minor losses, although one man, Lewis Allen of Company I, died of his wounds two weeks later; another was wounded.[186]

On February 9, Private Francis H. Stahle of Company B from Adams County was on a typical shift of picket duty. That night, however, he decided to take the guard's horses outside the picket line to find water. In moments, he was ambushed and killed. His remains were returned to the family, and

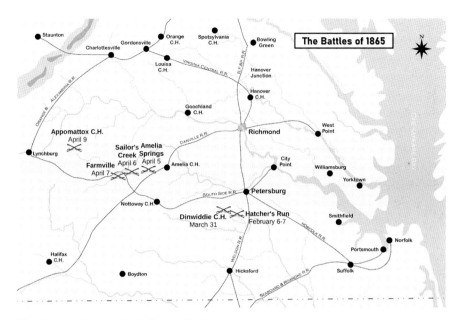

The Battles of 1865. *Map by Britt C. Isenberg.*

he was interred at Gettysburg's Evergreen Cemetery. The continual danger, even on such seemingly innocent missions, struck fear into every soldier.[187]

During the last week of February, the 21st Pennsylvania Cavalry was transferred from the Third Brigade to the Second Brigade, which was commanded by veteran Colonel John Irvin Gregg. They were all Pennsylvanians and, in some cases, shared common homes. The brigade was as experienced as its commander and consisted of the 4th, 8th and 16th Pennsylvania Cavalry with Batteries H and I of the 1st U.S. Artillery attached.[188]

Abruptly, on March 2, the division commander, General David M. Gregg, resigned his post. The news came as a shock to the men in the ranks. By most accounts, they admired and deeply respected the brave general who led them through so many campaigns. His replacement was Major General George Crook, father-in-law to the late Confederate general J.E.B. Stuart and an old army veteran who struggled to find or inspire success during much of the previous four years. If nothing else, like all the men in the ranks, he was very experienced and prepared to meet the foe.

The weather slowly began to warm. The soldiers on both sides anticipated the start of the final campaign. However, most of March was spent in waiting. Army commanders wanted to ensure as much as possible

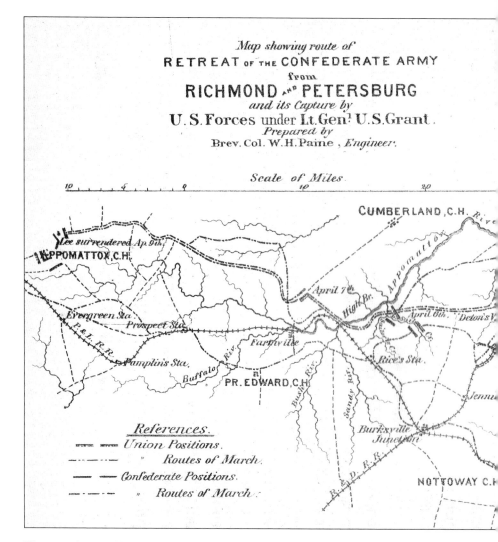

The ground covered by the two armies over the last week of the war. *Library of Congress.*

good roads for their planned movements. Many of the men were itching for the fight that was to come.

Finally, the day arrived on March 29. As Private John Sharrah wrote in his diary, "[S]tart on the Campaign of '65." General Phil Sheridan had command of all the army's cavalry, and his veteran horsemen started out at 6:00 a.m. toward what they believed was the enemy flank in the vicinity of Dinwiddie Court House. Within two miles of the small hamlet, they struck enemy pickets but quickly drove them northward. In the process,

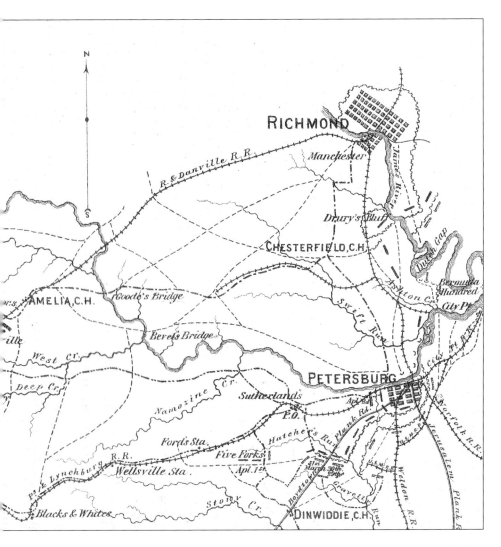

the 21st Pennsylvania captured two officers and nine men without suffering any casualties.

It rained for much of the following day, quickly transforming the roads into pits of mud. The regiment remained in bivouac until March 31. Early that morning, the other two brigades of the division were attacked north of the courthouse, and Gregg's brigade was called to the support of Davies's First Brigade. The men mounted and rode cross-country to the scene of the action.

Upon arriving, they found the regiments of Davies's brigade falling back toward the Five Forks Road. Gregg dismounted the 4th, 8th and 16th

Pennsylvania Cavalry and advanced them toward the sound of the heaviest firing. The 21st Pennsylvania missed the entire fight since it was on picket duty south of Dinwiddie. Shortly thereafter, its brigade mates collided with enemy troops belonging to General George Pickett's division. The objective now became to hold out until Sheridan could provide more support along the roadway, and they did. Late in the day, the brigade withdrew to the east, and a new line of battle was taken up just north of Dinwiddie Court House. The 21st Pennsylvania Cavalry rejoined the brigade that evening. The Confederates pressed cautiously against the new defensive line but halted their advance with the onset of nightfall.

By evening, most of Sheridan's cavalry were on the field and bolstered the line. To everyone's surprise, no Confederate attack came that night. In fact, they withdrew northward to the crossroads at Five Forks, which only emboldened Sheridan to press the issue the following day.

Leading a charmed story so far, the 21st Pennsylvania and the rest of the brigade were relegated to guarding the flank as the cavalry corps advanced north to rendezvous with Warren's Fifth Corps at Five Forks on April 1. It took time, but a powerful assault by Sheridan with assistance from Warren's infantry smashed past both Confederate flanks along the White Oak Road, sending survivors panic stricken in retreat northward.

The brigade was ordered to rejoin its victorious comrades the following day and marched past the scene of the April 1 action via White Oak Road and then Ford's Church Road. They reunited with General Wesley Merritt's division along the Namozine Road later in the day. All these movements must have blurred understandings of the situation for the horsemen, but their efforts were in effect stretching General Lee's line to the breaking point. For it was also on that day that Federal infantry broke the enemy lines just southwest of Petersburg. Major Bell wrote to his wife, "If you had heard the cheering yesterday when we heard that Petersburg was taken, it would have done your heart good....There are a great many [Confederates] giving themselves up as they think the whole thing is gone up, and I think so too."[189]

April 3 and 4 were days of marching for the brigade. The men moved along the flanks of the infantry and were called to a rendezvous near Sheridan's headquarters on the morning of April 5. Only an hour after arriving, they learned that Colonel Smith's Third Brigade was being attacked along the Amelia Springs Road south of Paineville. Smith's brigade had struck the retreating Confederate wagon train and destroyed two hundred wagons north of Paineville. In turn, they were counterattacked by General Fitz Lee's cavalry and forced southward back toward Jetersville.

Adjutant Samuel Henry of Cambria County made a narrow escape at Amelia Springs. *Author's collection.*

Both Gregg's and Davies's brigades were sent as reinforcements. Advancing to Jetersville, the troopers turned north toward Amelia Springs and found Davies's men being pushed back south of Flat Creek. The First Brigade withdrew, and Gregg's Second Brigade now found itself in front of Lee's angry troopers playing the role of rescuer. The entire brigade formed in line to resist the attack and, in most places, swiftly forced the enemy back from whence they came. However, a few small pockets of the Federal line were forced to fall back themselves and nearly cut off.

The 21st Pennsylvania's adjutant, Samuel Henry, was saved by a button on his vest. He had two horses shot from under him and took one bullet through the collar, although not a bit of skin was nicked. Major Bell was surrounded by three carbines at a distance of twelve feet, but neither he nor his horse was hit. Six other men of the regiment were captured.

The action was brief but desperate, and the losses support that. In less than half an hour, 31 men in the 21st Pennsylvania Cavalry were lost. Privates William F. Gross, Jacob Middower and John Suter were killed. Another 23 men were wounded, 5 of whom would die in the days and weeks ahead. Thanks to the timely support of Gregg's brigade, Davies's brigade was able to escape with much of its captured materiel, including eleven battle flags, artillery implements, 310 teamsters, 400 animals and 320 prisoners.[190]

There was no letting up the pressure as Sheridan pressed his cavalry to cut Lee off. Federal infantry was now also making significant headway to add weight to the nasty little engagements that continued to sap the ability of Lee's veterans to fight. Near Deatonville, the brigade struck the Confederate train again but was driven away by General John B. Gordon's men. Pulling back, they reformed and continued southwestward. They again found the enemy just north of Little Sailor's Creek. Smith's Third Brigade hit part of Confederate general Richard H. Anderson's Third Corps on the road to Rice's Station. General Horatio Wright's Sixth Corps was coming up behind the cavalry and deployed for an attack that they hoped might finally bring about the destruction of Lee's Army of Northern Virginia.

Gravestone of saddler Amos Shuey of Company H at Jonestown in Dauphin County. Shuey was wounded at Amelia Springs and died one month later. *Author's collection.*

Meanwhile, Crook's entire division swung to the southwest across Little Sailor's Creek with the divisions of Custer and Devin from Sheridan's Army of the Shenandoah. There was some delay in coordinating an assault, but the troopers dismounted and awaited the moment to charge. Near dusk, the Federals unleashed a powerful attack against the enemy's right flank while Wright's infantry smashed in the Confederate left to the northeast.

In General Crook's Division, General Davies's brigade advanced prematurely with devastating consequences. It reformed on the left of General George Armstrong Custer's division, which was then preparing to advance in coordination with the rest of Crook's division.

Colonel Gregg dismounted his brigade preparatory to the advance, with the exception of the 21st Pennsylvania Cavalry. It was kept to horse as the brigade reserve. General Crook then ordered Gregg to advance with Custer, who was advancing on the right. The other three regiments strode through a thick woodlot that Crook hoped would partially conceal their avenue of advance to the enemy's position along the road to Rice's Station. If they could capture this roadway, the enemy's escape route would be severed. The veteran Pennsylvanians charged, and shots rang out. "The strife now was in thick woods and at the very side of the coveted road; and the rebels found but a poor shelter in its adjoining rail fence. Nothing, however, could be seen, and as you listened to the mingling crash and din of small arms, it seemed that the dismounted troopers could scarce compete with such formidable infantry."

Colonel Gregg sent back an aide to Crook, who reported that his men had reached the enemy train and set it alight. Crook told the aide to tell Gregg "to push on, destroy all he can, and charge those rebels in flank and rear." With that, Colonel Knowles ordered the 21st to charge into the fray joining its brigade mates. It was the first of seven charges, according to a man in Company B. To the right, Custer's men were struggling to make any headway. Then General Thomas C. Devin's division joined the attack.[191]

Staff officer Henry Tremain witnessed the advance: "A bugle sounded, and as bugle after bugle echoed 'the charge' along that line of cavalry, there was one grand jump to conflict. All was dust and confusion; horses and men fell dead across the rebel works. Every firearm might have been discharged, but on one side all was desperation, horror, and dismay, while on the other, confidence, enthusiasm, and victory. The rebel line was gone, and squads, companies, and regiments were flying over the hills.... Troopers in blue rode fearlessly and carelessly among a motley mob in gray, and received their unceremonious surrender. All was excitement and irregularity." Caught in a giant pincer that finally achieved coordination, there was little the Confederates could do but surrender or try to run.[192]

About six thousand Confederate soldiers were captured that day. Among them were Generals Richard S. Ewell

Jacob Immell of Company L showing his wound from Amelia Springs, which proved mortal almost two months later. *Library of Congress.*

and Joseph Kershaw. On the Federal side, brigade commander Gregg was slightly wounded in the fight. In the 21st, Private James Palmer of Company L was the only man officially reported killed. However, in the melee Second Lieutenant J. Henry Triece of Company F from Blairsville, Indiana County, disappeared, never to be seen again. He was the second Triece boy to be lost in the war. John Brown of the same company also went missing. Major Robert Bell claimed there were only eight men left in Company F. At least five others were wounded. The brigade also captured two pieces of artillery discarded by the enemy when they began to run and took about four hundred prisoners.[193]

There was little rest even after such a decisive victory. Sheridan continued to nip at Lee until the army was bagged. On April 7, the brigade marched across the Appomattox River for Farmville and found the enemy again two miles from the village. "A wagon train was discovered moving in the direction of Lynchburg and cutting across the road on which Crook was traveling. The white covers of the wagons were partially screened by the woods, yet nothing more than a picket guard appeared to intervene. At the same moment a column of Rebel cavalry was espied moving with the train." The 4th Pennsylvania Cavalry of Gregg's Second Brigade pushed the enemy skirmishers back through the streets of Farmville and came within sight of the enemy's retreating trains. Davies's brigade was called up for support. However, it was too late.

Confederate cavalry commanded by General Thomas Rosser hit the 4th Pennsylvania in the roadway from two sides. Each successive regiment in Gregg's brigade attempted to respond, but there was no time to deploy. Major William B. Mays of the 4th was killed. Lieutenant Colonel John K. Robison of the 16th Pennsylvania Cavalry was wounded. Colonel Gregg and two members of his staff were captured. Major Bell of the 21st was also nearly captured but somehow managed to escape thanks to a good horse. Veteran First Lieutenant John T. Pfoutz of Company L was not as lucky as Bell and was hauled off by the enemy.[194]

The brigade was relieved that evening and went to Prospect Station, where it encamped just after midnight on April 8. The men finally received some rest, at least until 9:00 a.m. The brigade, now commanded by Colonel Samuel B.M. Young of the 4th Pennsylvania Cavalry, marched through Pamplin's Station and united with the rest of the cavalry corps near Appomattox Station, where it went into bivouac for the night.

On Sunday, April 9, the entire brigade was ordered to the support of the Third Brigade and cavalry under General Ranald Mackenzie from

Corps badge worn by a member of Company E. *Author's collection.*

the Army of the James. Both forces were falling back under the weight of combined enemy infantry and cavalry assaults commanded by General John B. Gordon along the Lynchburg Stage Road west of Appomattox Court House.

The 4th Pennsylvania Cavalry charged into the enemy first, eventually joined by the remainder of the brigade south of the roadway. It thrashed through the enemy columns. General Crook's Second Division received assistance to the south from General Wesley Merritt and Thomas C. Devin. The Confederate effort to break out in the direction of Lynchburg was ebbing.

Colonel Young ordered his Pennsylvanians to redeploy farther west along the roadway to continue supporting Davies's brigade. "The brigade was massed on the left of the road and pushed forward at a trot, when orders were received to halt and cease firing." General Davies also ordered a flag of truce out to cross the lines. Unfortunately, those orders did not reach the 21st Pennsylvania Cavalry and Colonel Knowles in time. The colonel "led his regiment in a gallant charge alone. Seeing that he was unsupported by the rest of the line, he halted, when the recall was sounded, and the four years of fighting in the Army of the Potomac ceased." The war was over.[195]

Six men of the regiment were wounded on April 9. Understandably, the climactic victory came with mixed emotions. "If it was not for the killed and wounded of the last few weeks," wrote Major Bell, "what a great thing it would be to look back to, and, my dear, I feel proud to think that I have had a hand in it." There was little more to say.[196]

Gregg's Second Brigade certainly played its part in securing the success of the army. Despite the fact that it received the least attention in any of the surviving sources on the campaign, the 21st Pennsylvania Cavalry suffered the most casualties of the four regiments in the brigade by far. According to the official records, 101 men were lost from March 29 to April 9. The second-closest regiment was the 8th Pennsylvania Cavalry, which suffered 62 casualties respectively during that same period.[197]

After the formal surrender at Appomattox Court House, the 21st marched on to Prospect Station, Burkeville, Nottoway Court House and eventually back to Petersburg. It was during this trip that it received the

Unidentified member of the 21st Pennsylvania Cavalry with a female companion. *Author's collection.*

disturbing news of President Lincoln's assassination. Everyone was held on high alert, and the death of the president only served to stoke fires of anger in the wake of the surrender at who should be, and how they should be, held accountable for the war.

By May, the regiment was dispersed in several different directions. Companies A and I went to Campbell Court House. Company C went back to Farmville, and Company G was stationed at Appomattox Court House. Company E continued service as the Sixth Corps headquarters escort. Meanwhile, the other seven companies went west to Lynchburg, where they remained until June 8. On that date, they were ordered to Danville. A week later, they were relieved by the 8th Pennsylvania Cavalry. The men turned over their horses and equipment and returned to Lynchburg.

On July 8, the 21st Pennsylvania Cavalry was mustered out of Federal service after two years in the field. The journey to Harrisburg took a week. From there the men dispersed to their homes. The agony of their experiences would reverberate for years to come, and they would only heal as the nation healed—one day at a time.[198]

Conclusion

A Soldier Who Would Surely
Return Blow for Blow

The Veteran Years

Although the guns were silent, the men of the 21st Pennsylvania Cavalry, like all veterans of the war, would never let go of their experiences during the bloody four-year conflict. Most of the men were eager to return home to some semblance of normalcy, whether that meant working the farm or plying their trade. They relished a hero's return to peacetime pursuits. The transition from soldier back to civilian, however, also presented many challenges.

Of course, many men never returned home to have such opportunities. During the regiment's entire term of service, 39 men were killed outright in combat. Another 38 succumbed to wounds; 113 died of disease and 3 died in Confederate prisoner of war camps. That makes for a total of 193 deaths in the regiment. Also on the casualty rolls, 215 men were wounded and 35 were prisoners or missing in action. Relatively, those numbers are quite high considering the regiment's total term of service was only two years.

Incredibly, Colonel Oliver B. Knowles, maybe the man most exposed to enemy fire during his soldiering career, was not once hit by an enemy bullet. Through his service with the Lincoln Cavalry in 1861 to the last charge at Appomattox on April 9, 1865, Knowles was vulnerable to capture or getting shot at close quarters numerous times, but the enemy was never able to bring him down.

The twenty-three-year-old had accomplished a great deal. Historian Samuel Bates wrote of him, "The conduct of Colonel Knowles throughout his entire military career, from that of a private carrying the carbine to his last charge when the foremost of all the Confederate leaders had been compelled to surrender, was most devoted and heroic, winning the respect and affection of those beneath him, and the confidence and admiration of his superiors. His unaffected simplicity of manner, genial bearing, and never-failing wit won for him troops of friends wherever he moved." For "Gallant and meritorious service," he was brevetted brigadier general. He was the highest-ranking officer borne of the 21st Pennsylvania Cavalry.[199]

Unidentified sergeant, likely of Company B; the image was taken at Tyson's photographic studio in Gettysburg. *Author's collection.*

Knowles returned home to Philadelphia and shortly thereafter decided to take up business in Milwaukee, Wisconsin, as a grain trader. Knowles proved himself a shrewd businessman. He did well for himself and his newly adopted city for more than a year.

On December 5, 1866, the general attended an exhibition with some friends at the city's Music Hall. Not feeling well, he left the show early. By midnight, several physicians had been called to his bedside, and it was determined he was suffering from cholera. The boy-general was told he had but a few hours to live. He wrote to his parents in Philadelphia and wanted them to rest knowing he did not fear death. As a new day dawned across the Midwest, Oliver B. Knowles passed into eternity.[200]

The general's remains were escorted back to Philadelphia for interment. Milwaukee's chamber of commerce passed public resolutions in his honor. A meeting was also convened by members of both Company C of the Lincoln Cavalry and the 21st Pennsylvania Cavalry headed by Captain James H. Stevenson. They, too, passed public resolutions of respect and sympathy: "Resolved, That in the death of our lamented comrade we deeply feel that we have lost one of the truest and dearest friends, and while we cherish the memory of his many excellent qualities we will strive to imitate his many virtues."[201]

Captain Stevenson wrote of Knowles shortly after his death:

As I gaze on the likeness of his youthful and manly face, I call to mind the many hardships and dangers through which we passed together, and his patient and soldierly bearing under the most trying circumstances. His goodness of heart was only equalled by his courage and patriotism....He was beloved by all the men, and they rejoiced at his success. He was more conspicuous in deeds than in words, and, recognizing this, his comrades rendered it unnecessary for him to sound his own praises. He had the talent to command in the midst of danger, and presence of mind to meet and surmount extraordinary perils. His presence seemed to dissipate fear, calm disturbed minds, and inspire confidence in the breasts of all under his charge. He had the faculty of enforcing discipline under the guidance of justice, moderation and good sense. Always yielding a cheerful obedience, he set an example to his inferiors which secured their obedience in return.

General Knowles was buried at Laurel Hill Cemetery in Philadelphia with so many other comrades who had gone before him. On his tombstone is inscribed, "He was: Gentle, yet Courageous, Firm, but Magnanimous, Beloved by all."[202]

Grave site of General Knowles at Laurel Hill Cemetery in Philadelphia. *Author's collection.*

Maybe the most notable of the surviving wounded men at war's end was the regiment's first commander, Colonel William H. Boyd. The bullet that struck him at Cold Harbor was finally extracted from a vertebra in his neck after five months and four separate, painful surgeries. He suffered from ill effects of the wound for the rest of his life.

The colonel returned to his residence at Federal Hill outside Chambersburg after his last surgery and slowly recovered his strength. He engaged in brickmaking, but later he frequently traveled to Washington, D.C., with the purpose of revamping his prewar success in the directories business with his brother. This eventually facilitated the family's permanent move to the capital. In 1868, Boyd became an agent of the U.S. Treasury. He was also named sheriff of Fauquier County, Virginia, in April 1869, which agitated one of the county's residents who happened to be a wartime nemesis.[203]

Famed partisan ranger Colonel John Singleton Mosby leveled accusations at Boyd that Mosby claimed were "not out of political differences, but mistrust for the man appointed to carry out reconstruction law in the county." The controversy swirled around Colonel Boyd's ability to provide a satisfactory bond. "We had no more notion of interfering with the reconstruction laws than you have," Mosby told a newspaper correspondent. "We simply wanted a man for sheriff who would not run away with the revenues of the county, or if he did run away we wanted to have some bondsmen that had something to take hold of."

Although Boyd was able to provide evidence of $30,000 and the district commander, General Edward Canby, reiterated Boyd's appointment, Mosby was not satisfied, likely because he had something to do with framing the illegitimacy of the bonds. He believed that "Boyd came here to swindle the county," although he could not provide any evidence.

Then the situation escalated farther when the two veterans met one day on a road near Warrenton. According to Mosby, Boyd turned his horse and said, "Colonel Mosby, if you don't stop interfering with my business I will make it a personal matter with you." Mosby's response was, "You can do so as soon as you please, and in any manner, or at any time." Colonel Boyd's blood was apparently boiling by this time. "Mosby, if you will go with me to Pennsylvania," said the colonel, "I will prove you to be a damned highway robber."

The correspondent from the *Richmond Dispatch* who interviewed Mosby asked him why he wouldn't fight Boyd. Mosby responded, "Well, I don't think that it is quite the thing for two gentleman who have served as colonels of cavalry to make bruisers of themselves. Besides, Colonel Boyd is a man of

Colonel Boyd through the years, shown with his brother. *Author's collection.*

about 175 pounds, and very athletic, while I don't weigh over 125 pounds. He could have crushed me in a fist-fight like an egg-shell." Regardless of reputational duties, Mosby knew well how to measure his opponents, as proven time and again on the battlefield.

However, Mosby created even more controversy. He told the correspondent that the two agreed to fight "at ten paces, with Colt's army revolver, the parties to advance as close as they pleased after the word was give to fire, and keep firing until all the barrels were emptied." Supposedly, some residents of Warrenton even spotted Mosby practicing for said duel one night in a ravine near town. It was a crafty move on Mosby's part, knowing full well that this accusation alone could cost Boyd his job simply by insinuating that he accepted the challenge of an illegal duel. Boyd also knew better and quickly accepted an offer for interview with several newspapers in which he flatly denied the claim.

The *Richmond Dispatch* was correct when it wrote, "Be that as it may, there is no disguising the fact the community of Warrenton regard Colonel Boyd as a coward. To live in Warrenton or anywhere else in Virginia and refuse to fight when challenged is to be called a coward, no matter what a man's courage may be." Boyd fired the closing salvo of what was, by that time, a very public dispute. His final letter was published by the *New York Herald*:

In regard to my own courage Mosby and his clique are incompetent to judge. It is a matter that is safe in the hands of my friends. But this much I may say, that I did not sneak through the country, plundering and marauding among the innocent and noncombatants. My character as a soldier is well known and understood through the Shenandoah valley, Fauquier and the adjoining counties. Mosby himself swore in open court he knew nothing against me, but has frequently heard me well spoken of by the people of that section, even though I was in arms against them. The assertion of Mosby that he never would have suffered the publication of the letters but that I boasted about town that he had backed down, is a base lie, and Mosby knows it. I defy any man to say I did so. I considered him too contemptibly small fry to talk about, and treated the subject with disgust. I had nothing to gain in associating my name with such scum.

In the end, Mosby eventually got his wish. Colonel Boyd returned to Washington and focused on his directory business with his younger brother Andrew. The Boyd brothers were successful at reviving business and expanded significantly over the following decade with the help of their nephew, Lieutenant William H. Boyd Jr. At its zenith, the company had directories for 175 cities and states.[204]

The colonel, entrepreneur, husband and father of six died on October 7, 1887. Tributes were printed in newspapers throughout his old haunts. The *Shippensburg Chronicle* wrote of Boyd, "He was the leader of many cavalry scouting parties when the war was transferred North of the Potomac, and he was as noble and chivalric as he was brave. He was well known to the enemy as their most tireless and dangerous pursuer, and how well he was appreciated as a soldier who would surely return blow for blow." Boyd was laid to rest at Glenwood Cemetery in Washington, D.C. His beloved wife, Elizabeth, passed away the following year, and side by side they rest eternally.[205]

The one unresolved matter more than a century and a half past is whether or not Boyd has the brevet rank of brigadier general. His gravestone at Glenwood is inscribed with the rank, and various other sources have been found offering the rank with his name. Unfortunately as of this date, no official documentation has been discovered through his personnel records. Even in death, a long-overdue promotion for the colonel remains somewhat ambiguous if not elusive.[206]

As Civil War veterans participated in every facet of the American life through the latter stages of the nineteenth century, age only heightened interests in remembering the deeds of comrades. After the war, Major

Robert Bell served as the cashier for the First National Bank in Gettysburg. He and his wife also had three more children. Life was surely busy, but the major's thoughts were never far from the war years.

Major Bell took it upon himself to organize and orchestrate the first reunion of the 21st Pennsylvania Cavalry Veteran's Association, which was to be held at Gettysburg on October 23, 1890, at the McClellan House. It certainly was an appropriate venue, but not only because Company B was recruited there. The majority of the regiment was raised in the adjacent counties, and Gettysburg offered a point of concentration, as it did on July 1–3, 1863. Major Bell paid for advertisements across the state with the hopes of attracting former comrades. One such ad read, "After a lapse of 25 years since the regiment was mustered out they think that it will do the members good to meet once more and fight their battles over."

Bell's efforts were a rousing success. Nearly eighty members of the regiment made the journey to Gettysburg. They established a permanent organization and voted Major Bell as president, Lieutenant William H. Boyd Jr. and First Sergeant Samuel M. Manifold as vice-presidents and R.R. Welsh and Lieutenant James T. Long as secretaries. Major Bell delivered an address documenting the history of the regiment, and then the members engaged in telling tales of their shared experience. It was determined that the next reunion would be held the following October in Gettysburg again.[207]

The second reunion was held on October 7, 1891, and was another rousing success that delighted the attending veterans. James T. Long served in Companies G and A during the war and rose to the rank of second lieutenant. It was thanks to his service with the regiment that he met his wife, Susan, while they were stationed in Chambersburg. By 1891, Long was well entrenched as one of the experts on the Battle of Gettysburg, and for that he received the honorary title of "Captain," even though he never received that commission during the war. That very year, he published his guidebook *Gettysburg: How the Battle Was Fought*, which was reprinted in many editions long after his death. He wrote another book, *The Sixteenth Decisive Battle of the World: Gettysburg*, which was published the year he died. Long operated his touring business out of the Springs Hotel beyond Willoughby Run on the first day's battleground. It was only fitting then that "Captain" Long led his comrades of the 21st Pennsylvania Cavalry in a tour across the battlefield for that year's excursion.[208]

There was little doubt that the reunions did the men good and that these events would and should continue. The Grand Army of the Republic

(GAR) was already well established, and many of the 21st's veterans had been attending fraternal events long before the establishment of the regimental association. However, the regimental gatherings offered an experience that post gatherings could not. Here they could spend time with the very men they marched and fought alongside. This facilitated more detailed accounting of events, and soon members of the regiment were requesting a regimental history or exploring questions about how to best honor the legacy of the regiment.

With each passing year, comrades were dying. Requests grew more urgent to achieve some form of appropriate remembrance in honor of all that had happened during the war for the sake of surviving veterans and future generations. Another reunion was held at Gettysburg, and it was determined that the association would pursue erecting a monument on the battlefield at Gettysburg. Furthermore, the State of Pennsylvania was providing $1,500 to each of Pennsylvania's regimental organizations that participated in the battle to place a monument on the battlefield.[209]

However, there were several challenges to overcome. Foremost was that the 21st Pennsylvania Cavalry was not officially the 21st Pennsylvania Cavalry by the time the battle occurred, although disparate companies were already in the field and serving during the campaign. Captain Long and newly elected U.S. Representative Thaddeus M. Mahon of Chambersburg corresponded with the U.S. War Department to facilitate the process of placing a monument. The War Department controlled permissions for placing monuments and approving inscriptions.

The veterans' association determined to place its monument as close as possible to the location of George Washington Sandoe's death since he was the first Union soldier to die at Gettysburg. Significant contributions by comrades, which included both time and money, helped to move the project along, although the War Department still did not issue any inscriptions. The regimental monument committee continually communicated with the Board of Commissioners on Gettysburg Monuments, providing any information it could to help more easily validate the regiment's service record.

By July 1893, exchanges were nearly at a standstill. Secretary John Page Nicholson at Gettysburg struggled to get the necessary evidence from Washington as several requests came back with statements such as, "It is regretted that this office is unable to furnish a reliable report comprising the information herein desired, the data therefor never having been compiled." It was as if, only thirty years later, the federal government had forgotten the role the regiment played in the war. It was also becoming clear that no monument would be erected before the next regimental reunion. Dr. Elias C. Kitchen, one of the regiment's assistant surgeons, "remarked that we were liable to die before seeing the monument." Many of Colonel Nicholson's exchanges were fruitless. Still, he persisted, and by September an inscription for a state monument had been drafted.[210]

The fourth regimental reunion was held at Chambersburg on October 4, 1893. Headquarters were established at the National Hotel, which was run by 21st veteran George Zullinger. The business meeting took place at the Housum GAR post. Major Bell spoke, and the veterans were serenaded by the Fayetteville Cornet Band. The association voted on resolutions concerning the well-being of comrades and determined to convene the following year at the same place. Officers were all reelected. The party then moved to the Chambersburg Opera House, where Congressman Thaddeus T. Mahon addressed the attendees and then introduced the keynote speaker, Dr. William D. Hall of Altoona. Hall served in the Lincoln Cavalry and was made an honorary member of the 21st Pennsylvania Cavalry association. To close the night, Lieutenant James T. Long delivered "his famous lecture on the Battle of Gettysburg, illustrating it with maps and stereopticon views. It was an interesting and instructive lecture and was concluded amid ringing cheers and applause."

Although the veterans could not dedicate a monument, the committee decided that it would travel to Gettysburg the following day to dedicate the cornerstone and base for the state monument on the site where George Sandoe was killed. Escorted by the Fayetteville Band, the veterans departed at 6:30 a.m. Four hours later, the cornerstone was laid, and Dr. Hall was again asked to offer an address:

> *On this historic field, with its hundreds of costly monuments testifying to the gallantry and heroism of the regiments who fought thereon, you have to-day consecrated this spot for the purpose of erecting a monument to the memory of George W. Sandoe, who was the first soldier to consecrate with his life's blood this field, dying in defense of the Union he so well loved.... It is an outrage that the National Government has not by its action said, here on this spot where was offered up Gettysburg's first sacrifice, have we in honor of this brave lad placed this memorial for all time, to teach the future generations true patriotism, rather than that you the survivors, his comrades, have to do so. I have been requested to speak of your two colonels, the lamented Generals Wm. H. Boyd and Oliver B. Knowles. I can not do so. My relations with them were of so close a character that feelings are beyond*

Veterans of the 21st Pennsylvania Cavalry with the Fayetteville Coronet Band on October 5, 1893, at the site of their future state monument. Major Robert Bell is standing in the center of the group, with Lieutenant Chandler seated just to his front right. Lieutenant and Gettysburg Guide James T. Long is standing at the very left. *Author's collection.*

my control. So simply let me say to you and of your gallant command, that under their guidance as your leaders, your keen sabres wielded by your sturdy arms, carved for you on the temple of fame, a record without stain or blemish.

Representative Mahon followed Dr. Hall with a speech of his own. At some point during the commemorative events that day, Gettysburg photographer William H. Tipton took a group photograph of the men posed around the foundation with members of the Fayetteville Coronet Band. Through aged faces, Tipton captured a fire still bright in the eyes of comrades once again united in a mission full of purpose…remembrance.[211]

Another roadblock to raising the monument carried into 1894. The veterans of the 21st Pennsylvania Cavalry wanted to honor Colonels Boyd and Knowles, which was at odds with the rules of the board. It was not appropriate to commemorate any one individual on a monument. Ironically, this notion was at odds with the very plan of the board to mark the spot where Sandoe was killed. Uncertain of how the situation might unfold and wanting to make certain a monument was placed, the regimental association began raising funds of its own volition. More than $1,500 was raised and a design was approved. It also settled on purchasing ground less than fifty yards from the proposed site for the state monument.[212]

Work was started on the regimental monument with hopes of being able to dedicate it at the next reunion. In the meantime, news was received that an inscription was approved for the state monument utilizing the funds from the commonwealth. This meant that two monuments would be erected within sight of each other, their purposes only slightly different. The regiment got its way in honoring their commanders, and the Gettysburg Monuments Committee approved a monument to its specifications as well, marking the spot where the first Union soldier to die at Gettysburg was killed.

The fifth reunion of the regiment was headquartered once more at Zullinger's National Hotel in Chambersburg and was scheduled to span two full days of activities. Comrades began to arrive on October 2, 1894, for the reunion's opening ceremony the following day. The attendance was reported to be the largest of any of the more than thirty years' worth of reunions the regiment would eventually hold.

Major Robert Bell once more called the association's business meeting to order on the afternoon of October 3 at the Housum Post GAR hall. Letters from absent comrades were read, the previous year's minutes were approved, roll was taken and it was reported that the monuments were ready for dedication the following day. The business meeting closed after voting on Lancaster as the host for the following year's reunion.

A party consisting of Major Bell, Lieutenant Boyd, Captain Long, Private Alexander K. Belt and Private Samuel Sherman took a carriage out the Pittsburgh Road west of Chambersburg to inspect their old campsite along Back Creek on the farm of George Grove. "The Major was anxious to see whether a roadway which had been cut through the bank of the creek to water the horses had been disturbed. It was found as it had been made, and will remain as one of the historical marks of the encampment."[213]

Lieutenant James T. Long in 1864. *Author's collection.*

That Wednesday evening, they held a campfire program at the GAR hall. Familiar faces offered words to the men with their families. Captain Long told the story of how he was captured at Chambersburg, "not by the enemy, but by a most charming young lady, who has held him prisoner ever since." Major Bell told stories, as did Lieutenant William H. Boyd Jr. "The company then proceeded to the basement of the Post hall where a sumptuous collation was spread, one of the chief features which was a seemingly inexhaustible supply of Pork and Beans." After stuffing themselves full, the veterans and their families retired to their rooms. There was still an important day ahead.

On Thursday morning, the association members traveled to Gettysburg and down the Baltimore Pike over Cemetery Hill and toward Rock Creek. There they were greeted by two beautiful monuments honoring the accomplishments of them and their fallen comrades thirty years before. The regimental monument was made of solid native granite. "On the front is carved a horse-shoe, within which is a horse's head, and below it are crossed sabres." The separate faces honored the regiment's service and were inscribed with concise biographies honoring Colonels Boyd and Knowles. It was at this monument that Major Robert Bell began the ceremonies. Representative Mahon was not able to attend, so Captain Long read his prepared speech to the audience:

> *From our brave Colonels, Boyd and Knowles, to the humblest enlisted man, all were brave men. No regiment has a better record for bravery and loyalty*

to the old flag. The officers were proud of their men, and the men adored and loved their officers. Together they stood in the red hell of battle, to save our Grand Republic. Since the war its members have lived the lives of honorable citizens. And the monument we erect in memory of the 21ˢᵗ Penn'a Cavalry, the inscriptions on it, will tell all who may look upon it of the love and devotion of its members to their country. Both Colonels being promoted to Brigadier Generals for bravery, an honor worthily bestowed on two as loyal and brave men as ever pulled a sword from its scabbard.

Once Long finished, the party walked the short distance to the state monument, where they had posed the previous year for William H. Tipton. They stood at the approximate location where Private Sandoe was killed on June 26, 1863, and unveiled what was "generally declared the finest cavalry monument on the field." With much less pomp and circumstance, a few words were said and the crowd disbursed.

In the reunion pamphlet that was later distributed to the regimental association, the following poem was submitted by saddler Charles C. Hassler in honor of the momentous occasion, although it dealt with another battlefield familiar to the men of the 21ˢᵗ: Cold Harbor. The first stanza could well relate the experiences they shared on many a field:

I visited that old, old field,
Where many years ago,
Together side by side we stood,
With anxious hearts you know.
For borne on every breeze that came,
From across that old field, Bill,
Came sounds that though long years have passed,
Methinks I hear them still…[214]

Major Bell continued to preside as president of the regimental association for the rest of his days. He lived out his remaining years with his wife, Abigail, on the family farm east of Gettysburg. From farmer to soldier to banker to historian, Major Bell's life was one well lived in service to his family, the country and his comrades. The major died two years after his wife on June 25, 1904. He was survived by eight children and twelve grandchildren. "He was a man of great kindness of heart and was ever charitable and generous to any one in need," wrote the *Gettysburg Compiler* upon his death. "A loving husband, an indulgent father, a true patriot and a good neighbor is the

Above: Veterans around the association's monument on the day of dedication in 1894. *Regimental report books.*

Right: Monument dedication ribbon worn by Private George W. Mowers of Fayetteville. He can be seen holding two grandchildren on his lap in the front row of the previous photo. *Author's collection.*

Above: The 21st Pennsylvania Cavalry state monument at Gettysburg in 1896. *Author's collection.*

Right: The 21st Pennsylvania Cavalry state monument today. *Author's collection.*

The 21st Pennsylvania Cavalry's regimental association monument today. *Author's collection.*

record he has left." Major Bell was laid to rest next to his wife at the historic Great Conewago Presbyterian Church near Hunterstown, only a few miles from the Bell farm at Granite Station.[215]

Regimental reunions continued with smaller and smaller attendance until at least 1920. Fifty-five years after the guns of the American Civil War fell silent, the living muster roll of the 21st Pennsylvania Cavalry was indeed much reduced. One common plea by veterans of the regiment throughout those postwar years was the desire for a regimental history, a record of their struggles and accomplishments for posterity. Although it has taken another century, that record is now again finally available to any curious inquirer. May the important legacy of these Pennsylvania soldiers and their families live long into the future.

Appendix

Casualties and Attrition

June 26, 1863, at Gettysburg, PA

<u>Killed</u>
Bell's Cavalry   George W. Sandoe

June 2–3, 1864, at Cold Harbor, Virginia

15 killed or died of wounds, 43 wounded, 1 POW (total: 59)

<u>Killed</u>
Company B	John Betiler
	Peter H. Mickley
Company E	Richard Waters, Second Lieutenant
	John Keating
Company G	John Smith
Company I	Daniel Wagoner, Sergeant
	David Parker
Company K	Henry Oyler

Died of Wounds

Company A	Edward J. Menear
Company B	George W. Conrad
	William Toot
Company E	De Forest Pratt
Company G	William H. Phillips, Captain
Company L	Freeman Scott, Corporal
Company M	Max Stohr

Wounded

Field & Staff	William H. Boyd, Colonel
Company A	William T. Shuler
	James M. Smith
	Henry J. Stern
Company B	Lafayette Brenizer, Sergeant
	Levi J. Hart, Sergeant
	William B. McNair
	Samuel A. Peacock
	Charles Prosser
	John A. Sharrah
	Jacob H. Weirman
Company C	James D. Bush
	George Houser
Company E	George W. Bowman
	David Buchanan
	George Cline
	John R. Greenawalt
	George McDonald
Company F	George W. Davis, Corporal
	John Maloy
	John W. Vancamp
Company G	Emmet D. Reynolds, First Sergeant
	Henry Lambert
Company H	James McClellan, Sergeant
	Daniel Kepple
	Theodore Parker
	Franklin Strauck
Company I	Martin P. Doyle, First Lieutenant
	Vincent M. Wilfong, Sergeant

	Hiram C. Edmiston, Corporal
	William H. Sutton, Corporal
	Austin C. Eckley
	Michael Geiger
	George R. McMullen
	Daniel H. Ney
	William Rhine
Company K	John A. Clark
	Edward G.W. Small
Company L	Jacob A. Sharrer
	Peter S. Stine
Company M	Christian C. Hager, Corporal
	Jacob Lear, Blacksmith
	George W. Pawlings

POW

Company G	George Clapsaddle

June 18–22, 1865, at Petersburg, Virginia

23 killed or died of wounds, 66 wounded (total: 89)

Killed

Company A	Daniel Heikes
Company E	Cyrus Holler
Company F	Airwine Horner
	Harrison Lohr
	William Pearson
Company H	Hugh Carr
Company K	Samuel Pike
	George Shaffer
Company M	Joseph Kendig, Corporal
	Simon Fitz
	Samuel Norris

Died of Wounds

Company B	Henry G. Lott, First Lieutenant
Company E	David Burkholder

Company G	William N. Bingaman
	George Smith
	Thomas Will
Company H	Daniel B. Bechtel
	William Minich
	George H. Reinoehl
Company M	John Armstrong, Sergeant
	Thaddeus Filby
	Frank Neil
	James Pennell

Wounded

Field & Staff	Richard F. Moson, Lieutenant Colonel
	Charles F. Gillies, Major
Company A	Hugh W. McCall, Captain
	Lafayette Johnson, Sergeant
	Joseph Smith, Corporal
	James H. Gordon
	Thomas A. Graham
	Michael E. Myers
	Charles Schroeder
	William N. Seitz
	Benjamin F. Walters
Company B	George C. Beecher
	Jesse H. Howk
	David W. Knouse
	Conrad Lynn
	William B. McClellan
	Nicholas Miller
	William F. Smith
	Noah Snyder
Company C	Jeremiah D. Kauffman
Company E	George Alexander
	Benjamin Merryfield
Company F	Patrick R. Markley
	William R. Marsh
	Jacob R. Miller
	Samuel Stutzman
Company G	William Cooper, Corporal

Jacob Keller
Israel Kyle
Henry Melcher
Elias J. Wilson

Company H   Edward Heckman, Commissary Sergeant
William W. Angline
James Bowman
David Burkett
Samuel Deininger
John Kepple
Isaac Lawrence
Jeremiah K. Lehman
Thomas McGongert

Company I   Abraham Bollinger
John Fisher
Charles Nichols
David Roush
George W. Whiteneck

Company K   Franklin Gamble, Sergeant
John McCormick, Corporal
Henry Ruthrauff

Company L   Isaac R. Crouse
Thomas Fannycase
Daniel Henry
William Myers
Samuel C. Stickle
William Stone
William H. Unger
Lewis W. Vanderau
Joseph Wilson

Company M   John A. Devers, Second Lieutenant
John K. Bair, Sergeant
Enos L. Wright, Sergeant
Thomas Dickerson
Thomas Hays
James W. Robinson
Charles Schezer
H.B. Williamson
William J. Wright

August 18–23, 1864, at Weldon Railroad, Virginia

3 killed or died of wounds, 7 wounded, 1 POW (total: 11)

Killed
Company G   Hugh Deihl
                       Milton Naugle

Died of Wounds
Company F   James Speer Orr, First Lieutenant

Wounded
Company B   Alexander K. Belt
                       Jacob H. Weirman
Company C   John Schrader
Company F   John W. Miller
Company G   Daniel W. Smith
Company H   Cyrus Schucker
Company I   George Rushenberger

POW
Company L   John Burrall

September 30, 1864, at Peebles Farm/Poplar Springs Church, Virginia

2 killed or died of wounds, 8 wounded (total: 10)

Killed
Company L   David Miller

Died of Wounds
Company I   William H. Hutchison, Corporal

Wounded
Company A   Emanuel E. King
                       William L. Winter

Company C	William E. Hack
	James W. Hoover
Company F	Samuel C. Best
Company G	Henry Pagan
Company H	Joseph A. Butt
Company L	George H. Deems

October 27, 1864, at Boydton Plank Road, Virginia

8 killed and died of wounds, 28 wounded, 4 wounded and POW, 3 wounded and missing (total: 43)

Killed

Company H	James Keller, Corporal
Company I	Harmon Way
Company M	James H. Weidmer

Died of Wounds

Company C	Lewis N. Soloman
Company E	Oscar F. Bowers, Corporal
Company G	Henry H. Groff, Corporal
Company K	Philip L. Gardner, Sergeant
	Andrew W. Scully

Wounded

Company A	Robert C. Ligget
	Conrad Snyder
	John Wilhelm
Company B	John W. Galvin (POW)
	Charles F. Hoffman
	Jesse H. Howk
Company C	Albert H. Bortell, Sergeant
	Jacob W. Price, Sergeant
	Franklin F. Charles
	Joseph B. McCoy
	William A. Miller (MIA)
	Samuel Otto (MIA)
	William W. Russell (MIA)

Company E	Henry B. Kendig, Second Lieutenant
	George Cline
	William H. Updegraff
Company F	John J. Benshoff, Sergeant
	Jacob M. Folson, Corporal
	Carson Swisher (POW)
Company G	William Chandler (POW), Second Lieutenant
	Nicholas Holtzhour
	Jacob B. Kugle (POW)
	John Quinn
Company H	George F. Cooke, Captain
	Henry C. Pearson, First Lieutenant
	Joseph Aulinbach
	Henry Mattus
Company I	Elias McMellen, Captain
	Martin P. Doyle, First Lieutenant
Company K	John M. Miller
	George W. Swisher
	Samuel A. Zumbro
Company L	John T. Pfoutz, Second Lieutenant
Company M	David Butzfield
	William Rohn

POW

Company I	Samuel B. Chilcoat
	James Shehan
Company K	William L. Smith
	William M. Starliper
Company L	Henry Keyser
	William Pine
	William H. Ridgely
	Jacob A. Sharrer
	Joseph Wilson
Company M	James Baird

NOTE: The Official Records of the War of the Rebellion show that the regiment lost a total of 57 men at Boydton Plank Road on October 27, 1864—3 men killed, 35 wounded and 19 captured or missing.

December 7–12, 1864, during the Belfield-Hicksford, Virginia Raid

3 killed and died of wounds, 6 wounded, 1 MIA (total: 10)

Killed
Company A   John Winter
Company I   Jeremiah Stoutzenberger

Died of Wounds
Company E   George W. Bowman

Wounded
Company A   John F. Burkholder, Quarter Master Sergeant
Company C   Wilmon Robinson, Corporal
Company H   William Grove, Corporal
Company L   James Fegan
               Otterbein J. Fry
Company M   John A. Devers, First Lieutenant

MIA
Company I   John Blair, Blacksmith

April 5, 1865, at Amelia Springs, Virginia

8 killed or died of wounds, 17 wounded, 1 wounded and POW, 5 POW (total: 30)

Killed
Company A   William F. Gross
Company F   Jacob Middower
Company G   John Suter

Died of Wounds
Company A   Aaron Knisley
               Daniel Myers
Company H   Amos Shuey, Saddler
Company L   Jacob Immell
Company M   Joseph Bivens

Wounded

Company A	Robert C. Ligget, Corporal
	David W. Craig
	William A. Kensley
	James Welch
Company B	Lafayette Brenizer, Sergeant
	Witherow D. Horner, Sergeant
	George F. Sites, Corporal
Company F	Peter W. Pike, Sergeant (POW)
	William Bowden
Company G	William Cooper, Sergeant
	John Bell, Corporal
	Joseph C. Lambert, Corporal
	John A. Howard
Company I	William H. Sutton, Sergeant
	George H. Allison, Farrier
Company L	John F. Harmony
	Matthew C. Wilson

POW

Company B	David Herring
	William Mickley
Company F	William Aschorn, Corporal
	Thomas A. Martin
	James N. Wilson

April 6, 1865, at Sailor's Creek, Virginia

1 killed or died of wounds, 5 wounded, 2 MIA (total: 8)

Died of Wounds

Company L	James Palmer

Wounded

Company F	Samuel Rhoades
Company H	Jeremiah Rebble
Company M	George Branthaver, Corporal
	Robert H. Long, Corporal
	Henry James

MIA

Company F   J. Henry Triece, Second Lieutenant

                  John Brown

April 9, 1865, at Appomattox Court House, Virginia

6 wounded (total: 6)

Wounded

Company F   William Livingston

Company G   George W. Kline

                  Emanuel Naugle

Company M   Patrick O'Conner, Sergeant

                  Isaac Worthington, Sergeant

                  William M. Burns

NOTE: The Official Records of the War of the Rebellion show that the regimental casualties were much higher during the final campaign of the war from March 29 until April 9, 1865: 4 killed, 25 wounded, 72 captured or missing (total: 101). Thus far the author has only been able to find 49.

CASUALTIES IN OTHER ACTIONS

13 killed or died of wounds, 24 wounded, 12 POW (total: 49)

Killed

Company B   Francis H. Stahle—February 9, 1865, at Petersburg, VA

Company G   Thomas Campbell, Corporal—August 3, 1864, at

                    Petersburg, VA

Company I   Jacob Keikel, Sergeant—March 21, 1865, at Petersburg, VA

                  Russell Ingalsby—March 21, 1865, at Petersburg, VA

                  Charles Nichols—March 21, 1865, at Petersburg, VA

Company K   George W. Frederick—July 30, 1864, at Petersburg, VA

Company L   Robert Cowels, Corporal—July 15, 1864, at Petersburg, VA

                  Andrew J. Martin—July 27, 1864, at Petersburg, VA

Died of Wounds

Company A	James T. Dorris, Corporal—July 18, 1864, at Petersburg, VA
Company I	Henry S. Carpenter, Sergeant—April 10, 1865, at Farmville, VA
	Lewis Allen—February 20, 1865, at Petersburg, VA
	John D. Knight—July 23, 1864, at Petersburg, VA
Company K	Lewis Ridenour—February 3, 1865, at Philadelphia, PA

Wounded

Company A	Thomas J. Collins, Commissary Sergeant—at Petersburg, VA
	Henry T. Burns—November 24, 1864, near Petersburg, VA
	Lewis H. Eppley—February 5, 1865, at Hatcher's Run, VA
	Henry M. Grass—April 7, 1865, at Farmville, VA
Company B	David Freed—December 4, 1864
Company D	David Chamberlain, First Sergeant—April 1, 1865, at Five Forks, VA
	Samuel J. Banker, Corporal—December 13, 1863, at Woodstock, VA
	Samuel A. Wickline—October 1, 1864, at Scranton, PA (accidental)
Company E	Edward A. Mitchell, Corporal—August 15, 1864, at Petersburg, VA
	John M. Blackburn
	Thaddeus M. Mahon—November 3, 1864, at Hatcher's Run, VA
	John Ream—September 6, 1864, at Weldon Railroad, VA
Company F	James Penrod—July 26, 1864, at Petersburg, VA
	Montgomery P. Smith—March 7, 1865, at Petersburg, VA
Company G	Hugh Hernier—June 24, 1864, at Petersburg, VA
	John A. Howard—August 8, 1864, at Petersburg, VA
	Joseph H. Taylor—February 6, 1865, at Hatcher's Run, VA
Company H	John Lamond, Second Lieutenant—March 31, 1865, at Dinwiddie C.H., VA
	Samuel Brenizer—December 1, 1864, at Stony Creek, VA
Company I	Henry S. Cott, Corporal—October 1, 1864, at Poplar Grove Church, VA
	Robert S. Gemmell—March 21, 1865, at Petersburg, VA

Company L   John H. Harmony, Captain—July 30, 1864, at Petersburg, VA

Jacob Kelley—September 15, 1864, at Weldon Railroad, VA

Company M   Abraham Myers, First Sergeant—December 1, 1864, at Stony Creek, VA

POW

Company D   George M. Foreman—November 20, 1863

Company E   George Alexander—December 2, 1864

Samuel Howard—December 2, 1864

Thomas McKee—December 2, 1864

Company I   Elias McMellen, Captain—October 1, 1864, at Poplar Grove Church, VA

Josiah Mentzer, Corporal

William A. Billings—March 21, 1865, at Petersburg, VA

Benjamin F. Deverter—March 21, 1865, at Petersburg, VA

David McDivitt—March 21, 1865, at Petersburg, VA

Mark Pugh

Company L   John T. Pfoutz, First Lieutenant—April 7, 1865, at Farmville, VA

Company M   Harry W. Blakemore

DIED OF DISEASE OR ACCIDENTALLY

(total: 113)

Field & Staff   Samuel M. Murphy, Assistant Surgeon—November 16, 1864

Company A   Daniel D. Pruner, First Lieutenant—July 1, 1864

David P. McAllister, Corporal—March 29, 1864

Jacob Hollinger, July 29, 1864

Henry C. Manifold—July 30, 1864

James D. Pell—July 20, 1864

Levi Smith—September 10, 1864

Benjamin F. Sprenkle—September 17, 1864

John Thompson—June 22, 1864

Company B	Thomas F. Black—November 15, 1864
	Luther G. Clapsaddle—July 20, 1864
	Oliver S. Hartzell—December 9, 1864
	George W. Keefauver—November 24, 1864
	Forrest D. Lynn—October 13, 1864
	Ross A. McKinney—July 17, 1864
	Jacob Ritter—July 29, 1864
	Isaac C. Rutter—September 8, 1864
	Jacob K. Sheads—October 23, 1864
Company C	Thaddeus S. Goodman, Sergeant—January 4, 1864
	Darling J. Vincent, Sergeant—June 25, 1864
	Lewis F. Kauffman—1864
	Adam S. Giner, Corporal—December 19, 1864
	Ulrich Baker—July 7, 1864
	Daniel Bear—November 3, 1863
	William H. Burris—March 31, 1864
	Franklin F. Charles—May 17, 1865
	John B. Elderkin—August 2, 1864
	Alfred D. Gladdin—May 20, 1865
	John Huffman—October 5, 1864
	Franklin Martin—May 17, 1865
	Aaron B. Meckley—November 4, 1863
	Robert Musser—March 1, 1864
	George B. Parsons—March 14, 1864
	Henry Sulley—July 1, 1864
	James T. Ward—December 22, 1864
Company D	W.H. Hockersmith, Bugler—August 15, 1863
	William H. Longenecker—September 20, 1863
	Andrew McKean—November 4, 1864
	John D. Wonderly—September 15, 1863
Company E	Elam B. Kendig, Blacksmith—October 29, 1864
	George A. Evans—September 19, 1864
	Peter Fry (accidentally)—May 30, 1865
	Casper Hugg—April 23, 1864
	William Walker—August 1, 1863
Company F	Daniel Benshoff, Corporal—December 5, 1864
	John Eichenour—July 19, 1864
	Charles M. Ellis (accidentally)—August 20, 1863
	George Gates—September 15, 1864

James K. Homer—January 9, 1865
Simon Hollibaugh—November 10, 1864
George Miller—August 28, 1864
Barnabas Moore—December 15, 1864
Samuel Potter—October 3, 1863
Alexander Walters—November 3, 1863

Company G William Shatzer, Blacksmith—May 9, 1865
David Estburn—October 5, 1865
John Estburn—January 11, 1865
George P. Heiner—March 9, 1865
Reuben M. Heiner—March 31, 1864
John B. Posey—September 13, 1864
John R. Sloan—December 9, 1864
Franklin Snyder—August 10, 1864
Elias Tittle—September 6, 1864
Gideon Williamson—December 31, 1864
William E. Wilson—December 10, 1864
Henry Winick—January 23, 1865

Company H John H. Snyder, First Sergeant—July 6, 1864
John J. Neal, Sergeant—1865
Richard Bower—November 16, 1864
Samuel Fix (drowned)—May 26, 1864
James Krick—October 6, 1864
Mahlon B. Pott (drowned)—February 12, 1864

Company I Hiram C. Edmiston, Sergeant—January 5, 1865
John Fisher, Corporal—December 26, 1864
William H. Bollinger—November 14, 1864
Henry S. Cott—October 19, 1864
Joseph M. Harley—November 22, 1864
Fidello Landon—March 14, 1864
Lewis C. Markley—March 28, 1864
Henry McFerren—September 6, 1863
John F. Romsey—March 23, 1864
William Shupert—December 16, 1864

Company K Humphrey K. Adams—June 13, 1865
Albert Alexander—September 26, 1864
Robert A. Connor—July 4, 1864
J. Wilson Hoover—December 17, 1863
Jeremiah Mummert—August 1, 1864

	William H. Raffensberger—July 16, 1865
	Henry Shrader—August 9, 1863
	William Wilders—May 23, 1865
	John L. Zimmerman—January 22, 1865
Company L	John Ausherman—October 9, 1863
	John Beesecker—September 26, 1863
	William Coldsmith—January 3, 1864
	William F. Heller—July 28, 1864
	George W. Hull—October 16, 1864
	James Imboden—July 12, 1864
	Cyrus D. Kerlin—March 10, 1865
	Henry Lane (accidentally)—September 20, 1863
	George W. Sheaffer—June 27, 1864
	William E. Vance—February 28, 1865
Company M	Henry Hinkle, Corporal—June 26, 1864
	David Barnhart—January 26, 1864
	Henry Fennell—November 4, 1864
	Jeff McClintock (accidentally)—December 25, 1863
	Henry McConnell—October 9, 1864
	John T. McGahuy—November 19, 1864
	Thomas Pugh—July 21, 1864
	William Six—April 16, 1864
	Henry M. Stoner—February 2, 1865
	Smith Ward—August 2, 1864
	William Ward—April 24, 1865
	John Worthington—September 13, 1864

Died POW

Company G	John M. White, Corporal—October 1, 1864, at Andersonville Prison, GA
	Philip M. Lutze—September 10, 1864, at Salisbury Prison, NC
Company M	James Baird—November 26, 1864, at Salisbury Prison, NC

Note: At least 17 men were wounded either before or after their service with the 21st Pennsylvania Cavalry serving other enlistments—the largest number at Fredericksburg in service with the 126th Pennsylvania Volunteer Infantry. Several who were wounded after service with the 21st died of their wounds. In the 21st Pennsylvania Cavalry, 77 men were killed in action or died from their wounds; 113 men died from disease or by accident. A total of 193 members of the 21st Pennsylvania Cavalry died between June 1863 and July 1865.

ATTRITION BY COMPANY

COMPANY	KIA	DOW	DODA	WIA	WPOW	POW	MIA	TOTAL
F&S	0	0	1	3	0	0	0	4
A	3	4	8	26	0	0	0	41
B	4	3	9	23	1	2	0	42
C	0	1	17	11	0	0	3	32
D	0	0	4	3	0	1	0	8
E	3	4	5	14	0	3	0	29
F	4	1	10	16	2	3	2	38
G	5	5	12	20	2	1	0	45
H	2	4	6	24	0	0	0	36
I	7	4	10	21	0	8	1	51
K	4	3	9	8	0	2	0	26
L	3	3	10	19	0	7	0	42
M	4	6	12	22	0	2	0	46
Total	**39**	**38**	**113**	**210**	**5**	**29**	**6**	**440**

Abbreviations: KIA (killed in action), DOW (died of wounds), DODA (died of disease or by accident), WIA (wounded in action), WPOW (wounded and prisoner of war), POW (prisoner of war), MIA (missing in action)

NOTE: This table includes only those men who could be verified through sourcing and the aggregate total is likely lower than the true count.

Attrition Among Commissioned Officers

Killed
Company E Richard Waters, Second Lieutenant

Died of Wounds
Company B Henry G. Lott, First Lieutenant
Company F James Speer Orr, First Lieutenant
Company G William H. Phillips, Captain

Died of Disease
Field & Staff Samuel M. Murphy, Assistant Surgeon
Company A Daniel D. Pruner, First Lieutenant

Wounded
F&S William H. Boyd, Colonel
    Richard F. Moson, Lieutenant Colonel
    Charles F. Gillies, Major
Company A Hugh McCall, Captain
Company E Henry B. Kendig, Second Lieutenant
Company H George F. Cooke, Captain
    Henry C. Pearson, First Lieutenant
    John H. Lamond, Second Lieutenant
Company I Elias McMellen, Captain
    Martin P. Doyle, First Lieutenant (twice)
Company L John H. Harmony, Captain
    John T. Pfoutz, Second Lieutenant
Company M John A. Devers, First Lieutenant (twice)

Wounded and POW
Company G William Chandler, Second Lieutenant

POW
Company I Elias McMellen, Captain

MIA
Company F J. Henry Triece, Second Lieutenant

Notes

Chapter 1

1. Stevenson, *History of the First Volunteer Cavalry of the War*, 41.
2. *The Official Records of the War of the Rebellion: A Compilation of the Official Records of the Union and Confederate Armies*, 128 vols. (Washington, D.C., 1880–1901), series 1, vol. 5, 15, 113–14. (Hereafter cited as *OR*. All references are to series 1 unless otherwise noted.)
3. Stevenson, *History of the First Volunteer Cavalry of the War*, 41.
4. *OR*, vol. 5, 114.
5. Stevenson, *History of the First Volunteer Cavalry of the War*, 42, 51.
6. Ibid., 42, 51; Philadelphia City Archives, Philadelphia, Pennsylvania, Death Certificates Index, 1803–1915, Jacob G. Erwen. Company C raised funds through a subscription to have Private Erwen's remains sent home. Captain Boyd personally escorted the remains back to Philadelphia and the young man's family. Erwen was interred on September 13, 1861, at Lawnview Cemetery (previously the Odd Fellows' Cemetery), Rockledge, Montgomery County, Pennsylvania.
7. *OR*, vol. 5, 113–14. Private Washington Lancaster later rejoined the company but was discharged for disability in April 1862. Private John V. Williams never returned to the regiment and was dropped from the muster rolls as a deserter, although it is quite possible that he was captured. General Franklin's official report asserts that both men were "thrown from their horses."

8. *OR*, vol. 5, 113; "Skirmish at Pohick Church," *Philadelphia Inquirer*, August 20, 1861; "Reports from Alexandria," *New York Times*, August 20, 1861; Beach, *First New York (Lincoln) Cavalry*, 37; "Death of Col. W.H. Boyd," *Franklin Repository*, October 10, 1887; Stevenson, *History of the First Volunteer Cavalry of the War*, 43–44, 65; Longacre, *Lincoln's Cavalrymen*, 54.

9. Bates, *Martial Deeds of Pennsylvania*, 880–81; 1851 Census of Canada East, Chambly; U.S. Census of 1870, District of Columbia, Washington, Ward 2, Family Number 308. The captain's parents were William Boyd and Ellen Brakey.

10. Stevenson, *History of the First Volunteer Cavalry of the War*, 13–33.

11. Ibid.

12. Ibid.

13. Secretary of War Simon Cameron authorized "Colonel Carl Schurz to raise and organize a volunteer regiment of cavalry" on May 1, 1861. In this order, he asserted, "The Government will provide the regiment with arms, but cannot provide the horses and equipments. For these necessaries we rely upon the patriotism of the States, and the citizens." This lack of particular state affiliation during recruitment because of Cameron's orders seems to be the culprit of later confusion among the two companies not from New York. Besides Boyd's Company C being composed of Pennsylvanians, Company K was composed of men from Grand Rapids, Michigan.

14. Stevenson, *History of the First Volunteer Cavalry of the War*, 33–39.

15. Bates, *Martial Deeds of Pennsylvania*, 614–15, 620; Stevenson, *History of the First Volunteer Cavalry of the War*, 43–44.

16. "Capt. W. Harry Boyd," *Pottsville Republican*, March 4, 1896. Many sources have confused Harry Boyd as the captain's son, an easy mistake to make since they share the same name. However, he is not. Captain Boyd did have a son with the name William Andrew, but he was born in 1850.

17. *OR*, vol. 27, part II, 111, 211; part III, 125, 162; "Scouting in the Cumberland Valley," *National Tribune*, October 7, 1909; "Gen. Milroy's Wagon Train," *National Intelligencer*, June 25, 1863; "Tyler's Wagon Train Ahead of the Rebels," *Lancaster Examiner*, June 24, 1863.

Chapter 2

18. *OR*, vol. 27, part II, 212, 217; Bradsby, *1866 History of Adams County, Pennsylvania*, 349; "Death of Major Robert Bell," *Gettysburg Compiler*, June 29, 1904.

19. Jacobs, *Rebel Invasion of Maryland and Pennsylvania*, 9; Haller, *Dismissal of Major Granville O. Haller*, 64–65.

20. Jacobs, *Rebel Invasion of Maryland and Pennsylvania*, 11; Haller, *Dismissal of Major Granville O. Haller*, 62–63; *History of the First Troop*, 72; Horner, *Letters of Major Robert Bell*, 8.

21. *Gettysburg Star & Sentinel*, July 29, 1883; *National Tribune*, September 6, 1883. A postwar newspaper later claimed that it was a soon-to-be member of the 21st Pennsylvania Cavalry who killed this first Rebel and named the shooter as Henry Hahn. Henry did not serve with the regiment, but there is a Conrad Hahn who served with Companies D and M. For a more detailed account of the action at the Cashtown Pass, see Mingus, *Flames Beyond Gettysburg*, 66–68.

22. Haller, *Dismissal of Major Granville O. Haller*, 62–63; *History of the First Troop*, 66.

23. Jacobs, *Rebel Invasion of Maryland and Pennsylvania*, 14–15; Haller, *Dismissal of Major Granville O. Haller*, 62–63; *History of the First Troop*, 68–69; "Killing of Geo. W. Sandoe," *Gettysburg Compiler*, September 27, 1905; Wingert, *Emergency Men!*, 66–67.

24. *Gettysburg Compiler*, July 6, 1906. Living near Gettysburg on Baltimore Street south of town at the time of the invasion was John Louis "Lou" McClellan. He later served in Company B of the 21st Pennsylvania Cavalry. McClellan was married to Georgia Wade, older sister of Mary Virginia "Jennie" Wade. Jennie Wade was helping take care of the couple's firstborn in their home on Baltimore Street when a stray bullet went through the home's north doors and struck her. She was dead within minutes, the only civilian killed at Gettysburg during the three days of battle. Interestingly, the Wade sisters' uncle, Thaddeus Filby, also served in the 21st Pennsylvania Cavalry (Company M). He was wounded during the initial attacks at Petersburg on June 18, 1864, and was discharged on account of his wounds. He died on March 28, 1865, and rests next to Jennie Wade at Gettysburg's Evergreen Cemetery.

25. Haller, *Dismissal of Major Granville O. Haller*, 62–63; *History of the First Troop*, 68–69; "Killing of Geo. W. Sandoe," *Gettysburg Compiler*, September 27, 1905; "Local Soldier First to Die in 1863," *Gettysburg Times*, April 6, 1999, interview of Debra Sandoe McCauslin. One account claims that Sandoe's horse actually did make the jump over a stone wall and "made a dash for the hill," which was probably McAllister's hill.

26. "Killing of Geo. W. Sandoe," *Gettysburg Compiler*, September 27, 1905; Porch and Boardman, *Elizabeth Thorn*, 10.

27. *Adams Sentinel and General Advertiser*, July 7, 1863; "Brilliant Record of the 21st Cavalry," *York Dispatch*, March 22, 1912. Like his neighbor, John A. Bell also began raising a cavalry company for the defense of their homes. Eventually, this command would become Company A of the 21st Pennsylvania Cavalry.

28. "Fight at Wrightsville," *Philadelphia Inquirer*, June 30, 1863; "David E. McGuigan," *Gettysburg Times*, January 19, 1926.

29. Haller, *Dismissal of Major Granville O. Haller*, 63.

Chapter 3

30. Beach, *First New York (Lincoln) Cavalry*, 248; Stevenson, *History of the First Volunteer Cavalry of the War*, 210.

31. "Where a Hero Fell," *Virginia Enterprise*, July 4, 1902; *Public Opinion*, August 3, 1900; *Buffalo Commercial*, June 23, 1863; Hoke, *Reminiscences of War*, 45; Beach, *First New York (Lincoln) Cavalry*, 248–50; Stevenson, *History of the First Volunteer Cavalry of the War*, 210–11. Corporal William H. Rihl was first buried where he fell on the Fleming Farm. He was then exhumed and buried at the Lutheran church in Greencastle. Twenty-one years later, he was again disinterred and buried where he fell. A twenty-one-foot-tall granite obelisk was dedicated at his grave site in 1877 and can still be seen on the west side of U.S. Route 11 a mile north of Greencastle. The community's GAR post was named in his honor.

32. Burkhart, *Shippensburg in the Civil War*, 25–26; Eunice Stewart letter to her parents, June 24, 1863, USAHEC.

33. Burkhart, *Shippensburg in the Civil War*, 25–26; Eunice Stewart letter to her parents, June 24, 1863, USAHEC; Goldsborough, *Maryland Line in the Confederate States Army*, 313.

34. *OR*, vol. 27, part II, 220; "Harrisburg and Carlisle Telegrams," *Lancaster Daily Inquirer*, June 27, 1863; "The Invasion," *Carlisle Herald*, July 31, 1863; Beach, *First New York (Lincoln) Cavalry*, 251–52; Stevenson, *History of the First Volunteer Cavalry of the War*, 212–14. For a full analysis of operations and skirmishes near Harrisburg, see *The Confederate Approach on Harrisburg* by Cooper H. Wingert.

35. *Valley Spirit*, July 8, 1863; *OR*, vol. 27, part III, 492, 508–9; "Scouting in the Cumberland Valley," *National Tribune*, October 7, 1909; *Philadelphia Inquirer*, July 4, 1863.

36. *OR*, vol. 27, part II, 220, 222–23.

37. *OR*, vol. 27, part III, 594, 623; Beach, *First New York (Lincoln) Cavalry*, 253; "The Invasion"; Stevenson, *History of the First Volunteer Cavalry of the War*, 214.

38. Bates, *Martial Deeds of Pennsylvania*, 617.

Chapter 4

39. *OR*, vol. 27, part II, 215–19; "Brilliant Record of 21st Cavalry," *York Dispatch*, March 22, 1912.

40. "Another Cavalry Company," *Lancaster Daily Inquirer*, June 23, 1863; "Capt. Vondersmith's Cavalry," *Daily Evening Express*, July 17, 1863; "Six Months Volunteers," *Daily Evening Express*, July 22, 1863.

41. NARA, U.S. Census of 1860, Drumore Township, Lancaster County, Pennsylvania, Dwelling Number 349; Chest Springs Borough, Cambria County, Pennsylvania, Dwelling Number 1737; PHMC, Death Certificates, Martin P. Doyle; NARA, Consolidated Lists of Civil War Draft Registration Records, Pennsylvania's 17th District, 63.

42. Alexander, *126th Pennsylvania*, 66–69.

43. NARA, CMSR, Colonel William H. Boyd; Horner, *Letters of Major Robert Bell*, 11.

44. NARA, CMSR, Lieutenant William H. Boyd, Oliver B. Knowles.

45. Bates, *History of Pennsylvania Volunteers*, vol. 5, 77.

46. PHMC, Civil War Muster Rolls and Related Records, 1861–1866, 21st Pennsylvania Cavalry Muster Rolls.

47. Horner, *Letters of Major Robert Bell*, 11.

48. Ibid., 14.

49. "Sanitary," *Franklin Repository*, August 19, 1863.

50. Bates, *History of Pennsylvania Volunteers*, vol. 5, 77; *OR*, vol. 57, 669.

Chapter 5

51. *OR*, vol. 57, 665–85.

52. Ibid.; Bates, *History of Pennsylvania Volunteers*, vol. 5, 77.

53. "Capt. Bell's Cavalry," *Gettysburg Compiler*, September 21, 1863; Coco, *Strange and Blighted Land*, 330–32; "Hospitals at Gettysburg," *Philadelphia Inquirer*, August 22, 1863; Horner, *Letters of Major Robert Bell*, 14.

54. Ibid.

55. PHMC, 21st Pennsylvania Cavalry Muster Rolls, Company F; NARA, U.S. Census of 1850, Johnstown, Cambria County, Pennsylvania, Family Number 167; U.S. Census of 1860, Johnstown, Cambria County, Pennsylvania, Family Number 644. Ellis's tombstone at Grandview Cemetery in Johnstown, Pennsylvania, lists his birth year as 1847. This is further corroborated by the U.S. Census of 1850 and 1860.

56. *OR*, vol. 57, 665–85; NARA, United States Census of 1860, Montgomery Township, Franklin County, Pennsylvania, Family Number 2224.

57. *OR*, vol. 57, 672, 675, 685; Center for Food and Public Health, "Glanders Fast Facts," Iowa State University, April 2008, http://www.cfsph.iastate.edu/FastFacts/pdfs/glanders_F.pdf. Glanders can be transmitted from animals to humans. Several men in the Scranton companies of the 21st Pennsylvania ended up dying from waterborne diseases that had similar symptoms to glanders, although it is impossible to prove.

58. "Brutal Murder," *Carbondale Advance*, September 12, 1863.

59. *OR*, vol. 57, 665–85.

60. Horner, *Letters of Major Robert Bell*, 15.

61. *OR*, vol. 57, 665–85; "From the M'Clure Dragoons."

62. "Fatal Accident," *Mercersburg Journal*, September 25, 1863.

63. NARA, U.S. Census of 1860, Chambersburg, Franklin County, Pennsylvania, Family Number 1289; Bates, *History of Franklin County, Pennsylvania*, 668.

64. "From the M'Clure Dragoons."

65. "All Hail to the Old Flag," *Franklin Repository*, October 14, 1863; "October Elections," *Lancaster Examiner and Herald*, October 21, 1863; "Pennsylvania Election," *Sunbury Gazette*, October 17, 1863; "The Elections," *Carlisle Weekly Herald*, October 16, 1863.

66. *OR*, vol. 29, part II, 330. General Darius Couch ordered Boyd to Sharpsburg with eight companies of cavalry. Besides his own five companies of the 21st Pennsylvania Cavalry, Boyd had three companies of the 22nd Pennsylvania Cavalry.

67. Stevenson, *History of the First Volunteer Cavalry of the War*, 233; Krick, *Staff Officers in Gray*, 230, 249; *OR*, vol. 29, part II, 411; vol. 57, 665–85; "New Commandant," *Philadelphia Inquirer*, November 9, 1863; "Movements on the Border," *Mercersburg Journal*, November 13, 1863.

68. *OR*, vol. 29, part II, 615.

69. "New Commandant"; "Movements on the Border."

70. *OR*, vol. 29, part I, 503–8, 517.

71. "From the Shenandoah Valley," *Philadelphia Inquirer*, November 19, 1863.

72. Stevenson, *History of the First Volunteer Cavalry of the War*, 214–15.

73. *OR*, vol. 29, part I, 642; Stevenson, *History of the First Volunteer Cavalry of the War*, 238.

74. Captain Stevenson reported that besides killing Private Black of Company C, Lincoln Cavalry, Sergeant Andrew McGuckin of Company C was also captured along with a man named Taylor from another company.

75. *OR*, vol. 29, part I, 642–44; Stevenson, *History of the First Volunteer Cavalry of the War*, 233; *Annual Report of the Adjutant General of the State of New York for the Year 1893*, vol. 2, 126. Hoagland is also spelled "Hoogland." The young trooper's remains were taken home, and he was buried at South Branch Reformed Church Cemetery in Hillsborough, New Jersey.

76. Stevenson, *History of the First Volunteer Cavalry of the War*, 239.

77. *OR*, vol. 29, part I, 642–43.

78. Stevenson, *History of the First Volunteer Cavalry of the War*, 241.

79. *OR*, vol. 29, part I, 643–44.

80. Ibid.

81. Ibid., 498–508.

Chapter 6

82. *OR*, vol. 57, 671; "Inspector of Cavalry," *Pittsburgh Commercial*, October 3, 1863. Lieutenant Colonel Richard F. Moson was appointed inspector of cavalry for the Department of the Susquehanna and detached from the command then in northeastern Pennsylvania for his duties at the state capital. It was a vote of confidence from General Julius Stahel but also underscored Moson's experience like so many officers in the 21st Pennsylvania.

83. Select Committee Relative to the Soldiers' National Cemetery, *Report of the Select Committee*, 3–9; Cole and Frampton, *Lincoln and the Human Interest Stories*, 6–10.

84. Horner, *Sgt. Hugh Paxton Bigham*, 6–8; Russinoff, "President Lincoln's Bodyguard for a Day."

85. "Consecration of the Soldiers' National Cemetery at Gettysburg," *Adams Sentinel*, November 24, 1863; Cole and Frampton, *Lincoln and the Human Interest Stories*, 6–10.

86. "Consecration of the Soldiers' National Cemetery at Gettysburg."

87. *OR*, vol. 29, part I, 935.

88. *OR*, vol. 29, part I, 936–37; "Brilliant Raid—Capture of Capt. Hugh Logan," *Franklin Repository*, December 30, 1863; *Norfolk Landmark*, May

27, 1898; *Lewistown Gazette*, January 6, 1864; *Hartford Courant*, January 2, 1864. Upon his release, Captain Logan returned to the Shenandoah Valley. He and his wife had seven children, and the captain lived out his life in Woodstock as a merchant. He is buried with his wife at the Emanuel Lutheran Church Cemetery in Woodstock.

89. *OR*, vol. 29, part I, 938–39; "Brilliant Raid—Capture of Capt. Hugh Logan."

90. *Adams Sentinel*, December 22, 1863; "New Grave Marker Dedicated for First Man Killed in G'burg Battle," *Gettysburg Times*, June 15, 1999.

91. *OR*, vol. 57, 671; Horner, *Letters of Major Robert Bell*, 15.

92. Sylvester F. Price to Abraham M. Price, December 21, 1863, author's collection; "Affairs at the State Capital," *Philadelphia Inquirer*, December 28, 1863.

93. *OR*, vol. 33, 5–8, 11–12.

94. "Confederate Officer Killed," *Richmond Dispatch*, January 12, 1864; Stevenson, *History of the First Volunteer Cavalry of the War*, 244–45. Whether Colonel Boyd confused the mortally wounded "Captain Armstrong" in his official report with Captain Blackford is not clear. No Captain Armstrong has been found on Confederate rolls as having died in January 1864. Boyd's report also insinuates that the events resulting in the mortal wounding of Captain Armstrong occurred at Winchester, not Newtown. Other facts align well with the details reported surrounding Captain Blackford's death, so it is not out of the question that Boyd simply confused the names and events.

95. *OR*, vol. 33, 11–12, 332–33.

96. Horner, *Letters of Major Robert Bell*, 15–16.

97. *OR*, vol. 33, 7–8.

98. Ibid., 371.

99. "Col. Boyd's Cavalry," *Franklin Repository*, January 20, 1864.

100. "Inauguration of Gov. Curtin," *Lancaster Examiner and Herald*, January 27, 1864; "Inauguration of Governor Curtin," *Philadelphia Inquirer*, January 20, 1864.

101. "Second Inauguration of Gov. Andrew G. Curtin," *Franklin Repository*, January 27, 1864; "Inauguration of Gov. Curtin," *Lancaster Examiner and Herald*, January 27, 1864.

102. Horner, *Letters of Major Robert Bell*, 16–17.

103. Ibid., 18; "Col. Boyd's Cavalry."

Chapter 7

104. Ibid.

105. Bates, *History of Pennsylvania Volunteers*, vol. 5, 77–97.

106. "21st Pennsylvania Cavalry," *Philadelphia Inquirer*, February 16, 1864.

107. "From the 21st Penn'a Cavalry," *Daily Express*, April 26, 1864; PHMC, 21st Pennsylvania Cavalry Muster Rolls, Company I; "Deaths Reported," *Philadelphia Inquirer*, March 25, 1864.

108. "Flag Presentation and Ball," *Valley Spirit*, April 6, 1864.

109. *OR*, vol. 36, part I, 12–18; Brands, *Man Who Saved the Union*, 298; Wheelan, *Bloody Spring*, 17–18.

110. Horner, *Letters of Major Robert Bell*, 21.

111. Samuel P. Glass to his wife, April 29, 1864, Appomattox Court House National Historical Park.

112. Stevenson, *History of the First Volunteer Cavalry of the War*, 260.

113. Black, *Lincoln Cavalryman*, 194.

114. *OR*, vol. 37, part I, 73; Stevenson, *History of the First Volunteer Cavalry of the War*, 264–70; O'Ferrall, *Forty Years of Active Service*, 94–95; Davis, *Battle of New Market*, 65–70; Black, *Lincoln Cavalryman*, 194.

115. Stevenson, *History of the First Volunteer Cavalry of the War*, 264–70; "More of Sigel's Expedition," *Pittsburgh Commercial*, May 25, 1864.

116. *OR*, vol. 37, part I, 73–75.

117. Stevenson, *History of the First Volunteer Cavalry of the War*, 270.

Chapter 8

118. *OR*, vol. 57, 639.

119. *OR*, vol. 36, part II, 802; "To Be Dismounted," *Pittsburgh Gazette*, May 27, 1864; Horner, *Letters of Major Robert Bell*, 23; *OR*, vol. 57, 639.

120. *OR*, vol. 36, part II, 907; *Pittsburgh Daily Commercial*, May 30, 1864; Horner, *Letters of Major Robert Bell*, 23.

121. *OR*, vol. 36, part III, 110–11.

122. Ibid., 145.

123. "21st PA. Cav.," *National Tribune*, April 15, 1909.

124. *OR*, vol. 36, part III, 666; vol. 57, 639.

125. Horner, *Letters of Major Robert Bell*, 23; *OR*, vol. 57, 639; PHMC, 21st Pennsylvania Cavalry Muster Rolls, Company H.

126. Meade, *Life and Letters of George Gordon Meade*, part II, 197–98.

127. Ibid.

128. "Local Intelligence," *Lancaster Daily Express,* June 16, 1864; "Engagement of the 21st Cavalry," *Mercersburg Journal,* June 17, 1864; *OR*, vol. 36, part III, 376–77, 453; Horner, *Letters of Major Robert Bell*, 25.

129. *OR*, vol. 36, part I, 86–87.

130. "From the 21st Cavalry," *Franklin Repository,* June 29, 1864.

131. PHMC, 21ˢᵗ Pennsylvania Cavalry Muster Rolls, Company E.

132. *OR*, vol. 36, part I, 565, 572; Parker and Carter, *Henry Wilson's Regiment*, 460.

133. *OR*, vol. 36, part I, 86, 565; "From the 21st Cavalry," *Franklin Repository*, June 29, 1864; MacNamara, *History of the Ninth Regiment*, 402–3.

134. *OR*, vol. 36, part I, 86, 565; "From the 21st Cavalry," *Franklin Repository*, June 29, 1864; Parker and Carter, *Henry Wilson's Regiment*, 460–61.

135. Penniman, *History of Franklin County, Pennsylvania*, 719; "The Casualties," *New York Herald,* June 8, 1864.

136. Horner, *Letters of Major Robert Bell*, 29; NARA, Soldier Personnel File, Emmet D. Reynolds.

137. "From the 21st Cavalry," *Franklin Repository*, June 29, 1864; Parker and Carter, *Henry Wilson's Regiment*, 461.

138. "From the 21st Cavalry," *Franklin Repository,* June 29, 1864; "Engagement of the 21st Cavalry," *Mercersburg Journal,* June 17, 1864; NARA, Personnel File of Colonel William H. Boyd.

139. Rhea, *Cold Harbor*, 372.

140. Captain Elias McMellen's unpublished report, August 4, 1864, author's collection; "From the 21st Cavalry," *Franklin Repository,* June 29, 1864; *OR*, vol. 36, part I, 170.

141. The Civil War Record of Henry F. Charles, 1862–1865, 16–17, Boyer Collection, AHEC.

142. "From the 21st Cavalry," *Franklin Repository,* June 29, 1864; Parker and Carter, *Henry Wilson's Regiment*, 463; *OR*, vol. 36, part I, 566.

143. Ibid., 566, 572.

144. NARA, Personnel File of Colonel William H. Boyd; Bates, *Martial Deeds of Pennsylvania*, 880–81; "Gallant 21st," *Franklin Repository,* June 29, 1864.

Chapter 9

145. *OR*, vol. 40, part I, 187, 463; vol. 57, 643, 658; "From the 21st Cavalry," *Franklin Repository*, June 29, 1864.

146. Fifth Annual Reunion of the Survivors of the 21st Pennsylvania Volunteer Cavalry (1894), 73; Parker and Carter, *Henry Wilson's Regiment*, 471.

147. Horner, *Letters of Major Robert Bell*, 30.

148. *OR*, vol. 40, part I, 455; Greene, *Campaign of Giants*, 178.

149. Fifth Annual Reunion of the Survivors of the 21st Pennsylvania Volunteer Cavalry (1894), 73–74.

150. *OR*, vol. 40, part I, 455–57; Samuel P. Glass to his wife, June 25, 1864, Appomattox Court House National Historical Park; *Adams Sentinel and General Advertiser*, July 5, 1864.

151. *Philadelphia Inquirer*, June 27, 1864; Fifth Annual Reunion of the Survivors of the 21st Pennsylvania Volunteer Cavalry (1894), 74.

152. *Adams Sentinel*, July 5, 1864; Greene, *Campaign of Giants*, 244; Captain Elias McMellen's unpublished report, August 4, 1864, author's collection; Horner, *Letters of Major Robert Bell*, 31–34; "Choice Poetry," *Adams Sentinel*, July 26, 1864.

153. *OR*, vol. 57, 655; "Gallant 21st Cavalry," *Franklin Repository*, June 29, 1864; "Left for the Field," *Bedford Inquirer*, July 22, 1864.

154. *Pittsburgh Commercial*, August 3, 1864.

155. Hoke, *Reminiscences of War*, 108.

156. NARA, Personnel File, Colonel William H. Boyd; "Rebel Invasion," *New England Farmer*, August 13, 1864.

157. "Highly Important News," *Baltimore Sun*, August 1, 1864; "The Campaign," *Charleston Mercury*, August 16, 1864.

158. "Wounded Officers at Home," *Franklin Repository*, August 24, 1863; Horner, *Letters of Major Robert Bell*, 39.

159. *OR*, vol. 42, part 1, 58; vol. 57, 637, 655; "Army Correspondence," *Bedford Inquirer*, September 2, 1864.

160. *OR*, vol. 42, part I, 123.

161. "An Infamous Outrage," *Intelligencer Journal*, September 20, 1864; "Mobs and Riots," *Northumberland County Democrat*, October 7, 1864; "Riots in Schuylkill County," *Lancaster Examiner*, November 4, 1863.

162. *OR*, vol. 42, part I, 58; part II, 1,000; vol. 57, 655.

163. Woodward, *History of the One Hundred and Ninety-Eighth*, 14–15; Sommers, *Richmond Redeemed*, 244–49.

164. *OR*, vol. 42, part I, 139; part II, 1,135.

Chapter 10

165. *OR*, vol. 42, part I, 98; Fourth Annual Reunion of the Survivors of the 21st Pennsylvania Volunteer Cavalry (1893), 53–54.

166. *OR*, vol. 42, part I, 83; "To Be Mounted," *Daily Evening Express*, October 15, 1864; "Twenty-First Cavalry," *Daily Evening Express*, November 7, 1864.

167. *OR*, vol. 42, part III, 98, 608; vol. 57, 637.

168. *OR*, vol. 42, part III, 317–18, 330–31.

169. Ibid., 340–41, 359.

170. Ibid., 366.

171. *OR*, vol. 42, part I, 608–9, 648.

172. Ibid.

173. Ibid.; Samuel P. Glass to his wife, November 2, 1864, Appomattox Court House National Historical Park.

174. "Handsome Compliment," *Daily Evening Express*, October 20, 1864; Horner, *Letters of Major Robert Bell*, 58.

175. "Twenty-First Cavalry," *Daily Evening Express*, November 7, 1864.

176. *OR*, vol. 42, part I, 609, 648.

177. Ibid.

178. Ibid.; Tobie, *History of the First Maine Cavalry*, 365. For a full description of the Battle of Boydton Plank Road, see *The Petersburg Campaign*, vol. 2, by Edwin C. Bearss with Bryce A Suderow.

179. "Twenty-First Cavalry."

180. "The Election," *Valley Spirit*, November 16, 1864; "Gregg's Cavalry Operations in the Late Move," *Nashville Daily Union*, December 20, 1864.

181. "From the Army of the Potomac," *Vermont Standard*, December 16, 1864; "Gregg's Cavalry Operations in the Late Move"; *OR*, vol. 42, part I, 611–13, 649; Tobie, *History of the First Maine Cavalry*, 372.

182. *OR*, vol. 42, part I, 612, 649; Horner, *Letters of Major Robert Bell*, 50–52.

Chapter 11

183. Harry W. Blakemore to Cousin Addie, January 7, 1865, author's collection.

184. Horner, *Letters of Major Robert Bell*, 56.

185. *OR Supplement*, vol. 57, 640, 650–52.

186. *OR*, vol. 46, part I, 371.

187. Diary of John A. Sharrah, transcribed by Mark Greenough, Appomattox Court House National Historic Site.

188. *OR*, vol. 46, part I, 592.

189. Diary of John A. Sharrah; *OR*, vol. 46, part I, 1,154–55; Horner, *Letters of Major Robert Bell*, 64.

190. Horner, *Letters of Major Robert Bell*, 67; Longacre, *Cavalry at Appomattox*, 129–32; Calkins, *Lee's Retreat*, 46–47.

191. Ibid.

192. Tremain, *Last Hours of Sheridan's Cavalry*, 152–53.

193. *OR*, vol. 46, part I, 1,154–55; Horner, *Letters of Major Robert Bell*, 66–67.

194. Ibid.

195. *OR*, vol. 46, part I, 1,155–56; Bates, *Martial Deeds of Pennsylvania*, 618.

196. Horner, *Letters of Major Robert Bell*, 66.

197. *OR*, vol. 46, part I, 1,156.

198. *OR Supplement*, vol. 57, 641; *Pittsburgh Daily Commercial*, July 15, 1865.

Conclusion

199. NARA, Personnel File of Oliver B. Knowles.

200. Bates, *Martial Deeds of Pennsylvania*, 614–21.

201. *Philadelphia Inquirer*, December 10, 1866.

202. Bates, *Martial Deeds of Pennsylvania*, 614–21.

203. "Death of Col. W.H. Boyd," *Public Opinion*, October 10, 1887; Bates, *Martial Deeds of Pennsylvania*, 880–81; NARA, Personnel File of William H. Boyd.

204. "Challenged to a Duel," *Valley Spirit*, October 20, 1869; "Rumored Duel," *Daily Examiner (San Francisco)*, October 28, 1869; "Interview with the Ex-Rebel Leader," *Richmond Dispatch*, October 18, 1869; "Mosby Anxious to Kill or Be Killed," *Philadelphia Inquirer*, October 5, 1869; "Letter to the Editor," *New York Herald*, October 16, 1869; Jones, *Ranger Mosby*, 283–84.

205. "Late Col. William H. Boyd," *Shippensburg Chronicle*, October 20, 1887.

206. Powell, *Officers of the Army and Navy*, 355.

207. Bradsby, *1866 History of Adams County, Pennsylvania*, 349; *Pittsburgh Dispatch*, September 28, 1890; "Twenty-First Volunteer Cavalry Reunion," *Philadelphia Inquirer*, October 24, 1890.

208. "Reunion of Veterans," *Harrisburg Telegraph*, September 21, 1891.

209. *New Oxford Item*, March 13, 1891; "Cavalry Monument," *Fulton Democrat*, March 30, 1892.

210. Gettysburg National Military Park, Regimental Files, 21st Pennsylvania Cavalry.

211. Fourth Annual Reunion of the 21st Pennsylvania Volunteer Cavalry, 42–64.

212. Fifth Reunion of the 21st Pennsylvania Volunteer Cavalry, 65–93.

213. "Gallant 21st Cavalry," *Public Opinion*, October 5, 1894.

214. Fifth Reunion of the 21st Pennsylvania Volunteer Cavalry, 65–93.

215. "Death of Major Robert Bell," *Gettysburg Compiler*, June 29, 1904.

SELECT BIBLIOGRAPHY

Archival—Unpublished Images and Manuscripts

Adams County Historical Society (ACHS—Gettysburg, PA)
  Robert Bell Collection
Appomattox Court House National Historical Park
  John A. Sharrah Diary
Sue Boardman Collection
Gettysburg National Military Park
  21st Pennsylvania Cavalry File
Michael Jones Collection
MOLLUS Collection
National Archives and Records Administration (NARA)
  Compiled Military Service Records (CMSR)
  Pension Records
  U.S. Census Records for the decades from 1850 to 1920
Michael Passero Collection
Pennsylvania Historical and Museum Collection
  Samuel P. Glass Collection
Paul Russinoff Collection
United States Army Heritage and Education Center (AHEC)
  Boyer Collection: The Civil War Record of Henry F. Charles, 1862–1865
  Raymond N. Clark student essay (1986), "Skirmishing Around Carlisle—1863"
  Samuel Z. Maxwell Collection
University of Virginia
  Franklin R. Rankin Diary

Official Documents, Reports

Annual Report of the Adjutant General of the State of New York For the Year 1893. Vol. 2. Albany, NY: James B. Lyon, State Printer, 1894.

Annual Report of the Survivors of the 21st Regiment Pennsylvania Volunteer Cavalry Association. 1893–1911. Author's collection.

General Orders of the War Department, Embracing the Years 1861, 1862, & 1863. 2 vols. New York: Derby & Miller, 1864.

Report of the Joint Committee on the Conduct of the War. Washington, D.C.: Government Printing Office, 1865.

Select Committee Relative to the Soldiers' National Cemetery. *Report of the Select Committee Relative to the Soldiers' National Cemetery Together with the Accompanying Documents as Reported to the House of Representatives of the Commonwealth of Pennsylvania, March 31, 1864.* Harrisburg, PA: Singerly & Myers, State Printers, 1864.

The War of the Rebellion: A Compilation of the Official Records of the Union and Confederate Armies. Washington, D.C.: Government Printing Office, 1880–1901.

Secondary Sources

Alexander, Ted. *The 126th Pennsylvania.* Shippensburg, PA: Beidel Printing House Inc., 1984.

Bates, Samuel P. *History of Franklin County, Pennsylvania.* Chicago, IL: Warner, Beers and Company, 1887.

———. *History of Pennsylvania Volunteers, 1861–1865.* Harrisburg, PA: B. Singerly, 1869–71.

———. *Martial Deeds of Pennsylvania.* Philadelphia, PA: T.H. Davis and Company, 1875.

Beach, William H. *The First New York (Lincoln) Cavalry.* New York: Lincoln Cavalry Association, 1902.

Black, Daniel P. *A Lincoln Cavalryman: The Civil War Letters of Henry Suydam 1st New York Lincoln Cavalry.* Hampstead, MD: Old Line Publishing, 2011.

Bradsby, H.C. *1886 History of Adams County Pennsylvania.* Chicago, IL: Warner, Beers & Company, 1886.

Brands, H.W. *The Man Who Saved the Union: Ulysses Grant in War and Peace.* New York: Doubleday, 2012.

Burkhart, William H., et al. *Shippensburg in the Civil War.* Shippensburg, PA: News-Chronicle Company, 1964.

Calkins, Chris. *Lee's Retreat: A History and Field Guide.* Richmond, VA: Page One History Publications, 2000.

Coco, Gregory A. *A Strange and Blighted Land: Gettysburg: The Aftermath of a Battle.* Gettysburg, PA: Thomas Publications, 1995.

Cole, James, and Reverend Roy E. Frampton. *Lincoln and the Human Interest Stories of the Gettysburg National Cemetery.* Hanover, PA: Sheridan Press, 1995.

Conrad, W.P., and Ted Alexander. *When War Passed This Way.* Shippensburg, PA: Beidel Printing House Inc., 1984.

Davis, William C. *The Battle of New Market.* Garden City, NY: Doubleday & Company Inc., 1975.

Duncan, Richard R. *Lee's Endangered Left: The Civil War in Western Virginia Spring of 1864.* Baton Rouge: Louisiana State University Press, 1998.

Furgurson, Ernest B. *Not War but Murder: Cold Harbor 1864.* New York: Vintage Civil War Library, 2000.

Goldsborough, W.W. *The Maryland Line in the Confederate States Army.* Baltimore, MD: Kelly, Piet & Company, 1869.

Greene, A. Wilson. *A Campaign of Giants: The Battle for Petersburg.* Vol. 1. Chapel Hill: University of North Carolina Press, 2018.

Haller, Granville O. *The Dismissal of Granville O. Haller of the Regular Army of the United States.* Paterson, NJ: Daily Guardian Office, 1863.

History of the First Troop Philadelphia City Cavalry. Philadelphia, PA: Hallowell & Company, 1875.

Hoke, Jacob. *Reminiscences of the War; or Incidents Which Transpired In and About Chambersburg, During the War of the Rebellion.* Chambersburg, PA: M.A. Foltz, Printer and Publisher, 1884.

Horner, John B. *The Letters of Major Robert Bell.* Gettysburg, PA: Horner Enterprises, 2005.

———. *Sgt. Hugh Paxton Bigham: Lincoln's Guard at Gettysburg.* Gettysburg, PA: Horner Enterprises, 1994.

Hunt, Roger D. *Brevet Brigadier Generals in Blue.* Gaithersburg, MD: Olde Soldier Books Inc., 1997.

———. *Colonels in Blue: The Mid-Atlantic States.* Mechanicsburg, PA: Stackpole Books, 2007.

Hyndman, Captain William. *History of A Cavalry Company: A Complete Record of Company "A", 4th Pennsylvania Cavalry.* Hightstown, NJ: Longstreet House, 1997. Reprint of the 1870 edition.

Jacobs, Michael. *Notes on the Rebel Invasion of Maryland and Pennsylvania and the Battle of Gettysburg July 1st, 2d and 3d, 1863*. Philadelphia, PA: J.B. Lippincott & Company, 1864.

Johnston, Angus James, II. *Virginia Railroads in the Civil War*. Chapel Hill: University of North Carolina Press, 1961.

Jones, Virgil Carrington. *Ranger Mosby*. Chapel Hill: University of North Carolina Press, 1944.

Krick, Robert E.L. *Staff Officers in Gray: A Biographical Register of the Staff Officers in the Army of Northern Virginia*. Chapel Hill: University of North Carolina Press, 2003.

Long, Captain James T. *The 16th Decisive Battle of the World: Gettysburg*. Gettysburg, PA: Gettysburg Compiler Print, 1906.

Longacre, Edward G. *The Cavalry at Appomattox: A Tactical Study of Mounted Operations during the Civil War's Climactic Campaign, March 27–April 9, 1865*. Mechanicsburg, PA: Stackpole Books, 2003.

———. *Lincoln's Cavalrymen: A History of the Mounted Forces of the Army of the Potomac, 1861–1865*. Norman: University of Oklahoma Press, 2012.

MacNamara, Daniel George. *History of the Ninth Regiment Massachusetts Volunteer Infantry*. Boston, MA: E.B. Stillings & Company, Printers, 1899.

Meade, George. *The Life and Letters of George Gordon Meade Major-General United States Army*. 2 vols. New York: Charles Scribner's Sons, 1913.

Mingus, Scott L., Sr. *Flames Beyond Gettysburg: The Confederate Expedition to the Susquehanna River, June 1863*. El Dorado Hills, CA: Savas Beatie LLC, 2011.

Newcomer, C. Armour. *Cole's Cavalry: Three Years in the Saddle in the Shenandoah Valley*. Baltimore, MD: Cushing & Company, 1895.

O'Ferrall, Charles T. *Forty Years of Active Service*. New York: Neale Publishing Company, 1904.

155th Pennsylvania Regimental Association: Under the Maltese Cross. Pittsburg, PA: 155th PA Regimental Association, 1910.

O'Neill, Robert F. *Chasing Jeb Stuart and John Mosby: The Union Cavalry in Northern Virginia from Second Manassas to Gettysburg*. Jefferson, NC: McFarland & Company Inc., 2012.

Parker, John L., and Robert G. Carter. *Henry Wilson's Regiment*. Boston, MA: Rand Avery Company, 1887.

Porch, Kathryn, and Sue Boardman. *Elizabeth Thorn: Wartime Caretaker of Gettysburg's Evergreen Cemetery*. Gettysburg, PA: Ten Roads Publishing, 2013.

Powell, Lieutenant Colonel William H. *Officers of the Army and Navy (Volunteer) Who Served in the Civil War*. Philadelphia, PA: L.R. Hamersly & Company, 1893.

Rhea, Gordon C. *Cold Harbor: Grant and Lee May 26–June 3, 1864*. Baton Rouge: Louisiana State University Press, 2002.

Russinoff, Paul. "President Lincoln's Bodyguard for a Day: Sgt. H. Paxton Bigham's Gettysburg Experience." *Military Images* 37, no. 3 (Summer 2019): 48–51.

Sommers, Richard J. *Richmond Redeemed: The Siege at Petersburg*. El Dorado Hills, CA: Savas Beatie LLC, 2014.

Spisak, Ernest D. *Pittsburgh's Forgotten Civil War Regiment: A History of the 62nd Pennsylvania Volunteer Infantry & the Men Who Served with Distinction*. Tarentum, PA: Word Association Publishers, 2013.

Stevenson, James H. *A History of the First Volunteer Cavalry of the War. Known as the First New York (Lincoln) Cavalry, and also as the Sabre Regiment. Its Organization, Campaigns and Battles*. Harrisburg, PA: Patriot Publishing Company, 1879.

Tobie, Edward B. *History of the First Maine Cavalry, 1861–1865*. Boston, MA: Press of Emery & Hughes, 1887.

Tremain, Henry E. *Last Hours of Sheridan's Cavalry*. New York: Bonnell, Silver & Bowers, 1904.

Wert, Jeffry D. *Mosby's Rangers*. New York: Simon and Schuster, 1990.

Wheelan, Joseph. *Bloody Spring: Forty Days that Sealed the Confederacy's Fate*. Boston, MA: Da Capo Press, 2014.

Wingert, Cooper H. *Almost Harrisburg: The Confederate Attempt on Pennsylvania's Capital*. Camp Hill, PA, 2012.

———. *The Confederate Approach on Harrisburg: The Gettysburg Campaign's Northernmost Reaches*. Charleston, SC: The History Press, 2012.

———. *Emergency Men: The 26th Pennsylvania Volunteer Militia and the Gettysburg Campaign*. Lynchburg, VA: Schroeder Publications, 2013.

Woodward, E.M. *History of the One Hundred and Ninety-Eighth Pennsylvania Volunteers*. Trenton, NJ: MacCrellish & Quigley, 1884.

About the Author

B ritt C. Isenberg is a native of Millersburg, Pennsylvania. As a public historian, he has conducted thousands of tours and programs encompassing various aspects of the American Civil War. He has also been a Licensed Battlefield Guide at Gettysburg National Military Park since 2014. Some of his programs have been featured on Pennsylvania Cable Network (PCN-TV) and CSPAN-History. Britt is the author of *The Boys Fought Like Demons* (2016) and coauthor of the book *Gettysburg's Peach Orchard* with James A. Hessler, winner of the 2019 Bachelder Coddington Award.